The Study of Politics

**FOUNDATIONS OF AMERICAN GOVERNMENT
AND POLITICAL SCIENCE**

Joseph P. Harris, Consulting Editor

The purpose of this series is to provide a group of relatively short treatises on major aspects of government in modern society. Each volume introduces the reader to a major field of political science through a discussion of important issues, problems, processes, and forces and at the same time includes an account of American political institutions. Each is the work of a distinguished scholar who is a specialist in and teaches the subjects covered. Together the volumes can well serve the needs of introductory courses in American government and political science.

ANDREW HACKER: The Study of Politics: The Western Tradition and American Origins

C. HERMAN PRITCHETT: The American Constitutional System

HUGH A. BONE and AUSTIN RANNEY: Politics and Voters

ROWLAND EGGER and JOSEPH P. HARRIS: The President and Congress

JOHN J. CORSON and JOSEPH P. HARRIS: Public Administration in Modern Society

CHARLES O. LERCHE, JR.: America in World Affairs

CHARLES R. ADRIAN: Governing Our Fifty States and Their Communities

THE STUDY OF POLITICS:
The Western Tradition and American Origins

Andrew Hacker

Cornell University

? If the index is correct, this book discusses two Americans, Hamilton + Madison — no more! Thirteen others are mentioned or discussed, from Plato to Marx.

McGRAW-HILL BOOK COMPANY, INC.
NEW YORK / SAN FRANCISCO /
TORONTO / LONDON

**THE STUDY OF POLITICS:
THE WESTERN TRADITION
AND AMERICAN ORIGINS**

*This book is set in linotype Janson. The
original specimen sheets date from about
1700 and are of Dutch origin. The chapter
openings are Century Bold Condensed and
the displayed heads are News Gothic Bold.*

Preface

This book is an introduction to the study of politics. Its intention is straightforward: to show what kinds of questions need to be asked for an understanding of the political life.

Part I summarizes the enduring problems of political theory, the great questions the Western tradition has posed and then sought to answer. These questions are best expressed in the literature of our political heritage, and at least passing reference is made to the books and authors that have contributed to this stream of ideas. But abstract ideas must be woven together with a knowledge of how institutions of government will function if men are to secure the ends they desire. Such a synthesis of theory and practice, probably the best yet attempted, was written at the birth of the American republic. Part II, therefore, discusses The Federalist, *the essays James Madison and Alexander Hamilton wrote in support of the newly drafted Constitution of the United States.*

The Federalist *contains a science of human nature, a philosophy of the good society, and an explanation of how the American political system would operate in this theoretical context. No less important, it shows that an enlightened understanding of the political life can come from men engaged in practical politics. If Madison and Hamilton were intensely involved in the problems of their time, they nevertheless demonstrated that it is possible to take the role of scientists and philosophers in the midst of a great ideological struggle. They form a model that any student of politics would do well to emulate.*

Andrew Hacker

Contents

THE STUDY OF POLITICS

Chapter 1

Basic to democracy is the right of every citizen to express political opinions. Men have fought—and are still fighting—for this fundamental freedom, and it is one that is never abandoned voluntarily. Moreover, each citizen creates for himself his own perception of political reality. That is, his view of politics is based on his own experience and preconceptions, and he is thoroughly persuaded that he sees things as they really are. The bank president and the garage mechanic, the bishop and the plumber, are all prepared to discourse on politics without much urging. Nor should this be surprising.

EQUAL VOTES AND EQUAL OPINIONS   In a democracy every adult citizen has the right to vote and thus to exercise a share of power equal to that of any other citizen. The public is asked to select the men and women who are to govern, a not unsubstantial responsibility. Yet no tests of knowledge or intelligence must be passed to acquire the vote. All that is required is to have reached the age of twenty-one, in some places eighteen, to have some semblance of literacy, and not to be a convicted felon or an inmate of a mental institution. Not only is passing an examination in political science unnecessary, but no evidence need be given that the voter has studied or reflected on political affairs. It is assumed that even the most average of citizens will know how he wants to be governed and who he wants to govern him. For, it has been observed, he is the one who wears the shoe and he knows where it pinches.

The citizen is flattered by this compliment democracy pays to him. (Some say the flattery goes to his head.) If he has the right to vote, the reasoning proceeds, he has the right to assume that his political knowledge is correct and his political opinions are sound. Woe unto the elected official who persists in telling his constituents that they are ignorant or misguided in their thinking. He may educate them to the acceptance of new ideas, and many politicians have accomplished this manful feat. But it is a long and cautious process, and such education must never appear to upset beliefs that are cherished or prejudices that are deeply held.

THE PLIGHT OF THE EXPERTS   Can a democracy have political "experts"? Can a society where the majority rules admit that there are, in its midst, persons of superior political knowledge? To grant this is to grant that there are some individuals whose opinions have more validity than those of their neighbors. This is a perplexing question, one that has concerned philosophers for over 2,000 years. But if it bothers the philosopher, it does not usually trouble the mechanic or the plumber. For, as has been pointed out, the average citizen is in no mood to give up his right to vote or to hand it over to someone who is supposedly more qualified to use it. By the same token he will not remain silent when political discussion is in the air. For he is unwilling to assume that his opinions are inferior to anyone else's.

Thus, the expert has a difficult time, perhaps an impossible one, establishing his credentials. For his audience (if he has one) is forever asking,

"What do *you* know that we don't know?" It is worth taking a moment to ponder whether there is a satisfactory answer to this question. The political expert is rare indeed who can persuade others that his researches have given him a superior knowledge of political reality. And he is hard pressed to convince others that his opinions on the rightness or wrongness of political policies are somehow sounder than those conventionally held. The audience is skeptical, and often a little annoyed, at such pretensions. For they know that although the expert may be smart, he has only one vote. His expertise brings no extra power, and seldom prestige, in the public mind.

UNLEARNING THE OBVIOUS   All this needs to be underlined because every year several hundred thousand Americans enroll in courses in political science. In doing this they are embarking on a process whereby they will become substantially more expert on the subject of politics than the average citizen. What are they about to learn?

They are, first and foremost, unlearning. They will discover very early in the season that the knowledge and opinions they have brought to college are highly unreliable. We are all, no matter what our backgrounds, raised in a comfortable and comforting world of illusions. We see only what we want to see and we believe what we want to believe. (Psychologists call this "selective perception.") An academic setting is the best place to dispel these illusions. For the college student is, for all intents and purposes, in a period of suspended animation. Father does not sit at the head of the dinner table each evening, handing down authoritative dicta on the latest mischiefs perpetrated by the men who govern us. There are not the Sunday visits of Uncle Jim, a successful businessman who seems to know all about what Congress should do and the Supreme Court should not do. In the place of Father and Uncle Jim are professors—men and women with new ideas that are bound to run counter to those that prevailed at home. Furthermore, the college student has several years of freedom before he must begin to support himself by earning a living. This is a welcome respite, not least for the purpose of developing an understanding of politics. For once one is in possession of a wife (or a husband), a family (or a job), the inevitable tendency is to view politics as it affects one's immediate interests. If an objective view once existed, it is replaced by subjective interpretations of politicians and policies. The citizen who is weighted down with personal responsibilities and ambitions is apt to draw political generalizations from his own needs and immediate experiences. In other words, he is prone to assume that the program which benefits him is the best one for the whole nation.

OVERCOMING IDEOLOGY The college setting is, to be sure, a sheltered one. But it is a shelter from the prejudices of the family dinner table and the interests that become ingrained later in life. Perhaps the best way to describe the problem is to say that most political knowledge and most political opinions are actually *ideology*. This term requires some explanation.

Ideology takes two forms. On the one hand, an ideology is a *distorted* perception of political reality. An individual may believe that his knowledge of politics is altogether accurate, that things are as he thinks them to be. But his perception is all too frequently a distorted one. It is unrealistic because he gets his information from newspapers, magazines, television programs, and acquaintances—all of whom tell him what he wants to hear. Everyone, for example, has a notion of what life is like in Communist China. Or everyone assumes he knows whether or not unemployment is a serious problem at this moment. But how many of us really know how many people have been executed or imprisoned in China, or how many people are actually out of work in our own country? The odds are that few have such information. Nevertheless we continue to assume that our knowledge of these conditions is correct knowledge. In other words, the pictures in our heads are ideologies. They are distorted images of reality, a reality we are unable or unwilling to see.

On the other hand, ideology is a *rationalization* of political arrangements we would either like to see continued or would like to see come into being. Man is a fascinating creature, and not the least of his charms is his ability to rationalize. You come across Jones hitting Smith over the head with a lead pipe. You ask Jones why he is so intent on making a dent in Smith's cranium. Does he reply, "I am doing this because it gives me pleasure"? Not at all. Jones explains to you in great detail why the lead pipe treatment is actually for Smith's own good—whether Smith realizes it or not. And our political discourse runs along similar ideological lines. We persuade ourselves that policies beneficial to ourselves augment the welfare of the entire country. A businessman asserts that he must be allowed greater profits so he can invest in the stock market, thus contributing to the nation's economic growth. The trade unionist, on the other hand, asks for a substantial raise in wages, claiming that his increased purchasing power will create more jobs and hence make for a prosperous economy. In actual fact the businessman wants the extra cash for a Florida vacation and the trade unionist wants his raise for similar, if less extravagant, reasons. But for each to get what he wants he must persuade others that these wants spring from lofty motives. So they invent rationalizations. If truth be known, then, most talk of "principles" is at the level of ideology. Hopefully a few people will divest themselves of their interests and emotions, at least temporarily, and thus be able to discuss the general good in an objective fashion.

IS POLITICS A SCIENCE?

The study of politics involves acquiring specialized knowledge. This knowledge, if it is to be taken seriously, cannot be secured in a haphazard way. As has been pointed out, the average person's store of political information comes from his "selective perception" of the events and personalities around him. Relying on the facts that seem to him most significant, he will conclude that labor unions are corrupt or that the Republican party is dominated by big business or that nuclear explosions cause cancer. But generalizations such as these are distortions of reality. Accurate political knowledge can only result from a systematic exploration of political life.

The study of politics is not a "science" in the sense that chemistry, physics, and biology are. The traditional sciences rely on controlled experiments, conducted in a laboratory setting. It is not possible to place politicians in a laboratory as if they were guinea pigs, nor is it possible to impose precise laboratory conditions on the political arenas of real life. (Imagine asking a candidate to "experiment" in his use of various campaign techniques, to see if perhaps some might be dispensed with. His reply will show that politicians have no desire to run in experimental mazes.) Moreover, the chemist or biologist can take a neutral or dispassionate view toward the materials with which he works. The amoeba and the atom can be regarded disinterestedly, the scientist having no emotional interest in whether they wiggle or split or lie still. The student of politics, on the other hand, may find himself deeply involved with his subject matter. Whether he acknowledges the fact or not, he will look on some people and policies as good and on others as evil. Such emotional involvement is bound to make many of his conclusions subjective rather than objective in character.

The term "political science" must therefore be used in a rather loose way. But not too loosely. The real question is which facts, and what arrangements of facts, are admissible in drawing conclusions. To say that one gathers and organizes facts in a systematic (or "scientific") way is to say that the *method* one uses is important.

SCIENCE IN THE SECOND WARD   The second ward in Central City is strongly Democratic. In the last election the Democratic candidate received 82 per cent of the votes. Smith and Jones, two political scientists, want to find out why the residents of the second ward are so enthusiastic in their support of the Democratic party. There are 10 square blocks in the ward, each block containing approximately 100 voters. Therefore Smith undertakes to study five blocks and Jones the other five. But before embarking on their joint project they must make several decisions on method. There are 500 voters in each half of the ward, clearly too many for one man to interview. So Smith and Jones decide that each will interview 50 people. Which 50? They agree upon a uniform method of sampling. They must also decide what questions to ask. For if they had not agreed beforehand, Smith might gather some information that Jones' interviews omitted. They may even draw up identical lists of questions.

In sum, Smith and Jones are ensuring that in using similar approaches they will obtain the same order of information as each proceeds with his part of the research. Furthermore, the facts they gather on voting behavior in the second ward will not be random impressions but rather systematic data on political behavior. It may be assumed that two other political scientists, Brown and Green, could do a subsequent survey of the second ward and if they followed the Smith-Jones method they would come up with much the same conclusions that Smith and Jones did. This is not to say that the second ward can be turned into a scientific laboratory. But it is to suggest that some experimental methods can be used in the study of living people and their political behavior.

FACTS OR VALUES?   Furthermore, suppose that Smith and Jones, the first team of researchers, were themselves supporters of the Democratic party. They might, probably unconsciously, tend to look on the second ward as a "good" neighborhood. They would regard the voting behavior of the residents as rational, and they would put the best construction on the answers they heard. Thus the conclusion of Smith and Jones' research might be that the second ward votes Democratic because it is composed of underpaid industrial workers who are using the political process as a means of bettering their condition.

Brown and Green, on the other hand, are Republicans. In their study of the second ward they might use exactly the same sampling and interviewing methods as Smith and Jones—and yet gain a different perception of the neighborhood. The answers they hear may tell them that the second ward voters are irrational and probably misguided. They will conclude that the residents may be poor and uneducated; but they are also shiftless and ignorant, and in all likelihood have been stirred into discontent by outside agitators.

Which assessment is the correct one? Smith and Jones, on the one hand, and Brown and Green, on the other, were all guilty of allowing their own values to intrude in their research. Although some of their conclusions may be interesting, they are all but partial depictions of the reality that is the second ward. There are several ways to prevent the intrusion of subjectivity. The first is for the student himself to become conscious of his own opinions and preferences. Then he can constantly ask himself if he is seeing what he wants to see or whether he is seeing what is really there. Most people do not have such an insight into their own prejudices, but a serious student of politics must develop this self-awareness. The second way is to check and recheck one's facts and conclusions with other students. This is why scholars write and publish their findings: so that their colleagues may read of their research and compare it with their own experience. Colleagues will be quick to point out the value assumptions that underlie a study. They will point to factors that have been omitted and to others that have been given exaggerated significance. All science, then, is "social" in that scientific truth requires agreement among the community of scholars who comprise a profession. On some questions there will never be agreement, for the facts present different conclusions to different observers. However, the aim of systematic study is to enlarge the area of agreed-upon knowledge and to reduce the realm of controversy.

POLITICAL PHILOSOPHY

Not all students of politics confine themselves to the quest for factual knowledge. Others are concerned with the search for *moral* knowledge. These political philosophers are interested not so much in how people and governments behave as they are in how they ought to behave. If the political scientist studies reality and tries to explain its functioning, the political philosopher studies ideas and tries to discover which have the greatest moral validity.

"THE GREAT BOOKS" Most of the great political philosophers are long since dead. The first great political thinker was Plato, who died in 347 B.C. Since his time there have been no more than 20 or 25 writers whose ideas have endured through history. Yet the books that flowed from the pens of these authors can provide a lifetime's reading for the student of political philosophy. Plato's *Republic*, for example, is only several hundred pages long. It is a depiction of an imaginary society, a utopia, organized in such a way that the ideal of justice is made actual. In this book Plato constructs a philosophy of human nature, social structure, political leadership, and the good life. The *Republic* is a book to be argued with, and men have been doing just that for well over a thousand years. One question is whether or not Plato's utopia is a totalitarian society, where human liberty is denied and authority exalted. To discuss such a problem it is necessary to read and reread the *Republic* with great care, asking what it was the author meant to say and why he framed his argument as he did. An understanding of Plato and the other great writers is fundamental to the study of political philosophy.

This is because the works of Plato—and of Aristotle, St. Thomas Aquinas, Niccolo Machiavelli, Thomas Hobbes, John Locke, Jean-Jacques Rousseau, Edmund Burke, Jeremy Bentham, G. W. F. Hegel, Karl Marx, and John Stuart Mill—all deal with the perennial questions of politics. They asked such questions as:

> What is justice?
> When should citizens obey the state?
> Are men equal?
> What makes authority legitimate?
> What is freedom?
> Is man good or evil?
> Is self-government possible?
> Are there laws of history?
> Which is prior: society or the individual?

These are moral questions, and there is more than one answer to each of them. Rousseau says that men are equal, and Burke would deny that proposition. Hegel asserts that society is more important than the individual, and Mill replies that the individual is prior to society.

The "great books," therefore, provide the best starting point for the study of the moral aspects of political life. The works of these authors endure because they dealt with fundamental questions, with problems that persist over time and which cross national boundaries. Not every generation or even every century produces a writer of the intellectual power of a Thomas Hobbes or a Jean-Jacques Rousseau. Indeed, we cannot say for sure if there are writers of their stature living among us right now. For it takes the passage of years, the test of time, before we know whether a political philosophy is destined to be of lasting value.

PHILOSOPHY OR OPINION? Go to the citizens of the second ward of Central City and ask them a simple question: Of all the countries in the world today, which is the "best"? If they want to know what you are driving at, explain that you want their judgment on which country offers the best life to its inhabitants, which country best satisfies the expectations of its citizens. It is easy to predict that you will get the same answer everywhere you go in the second ward. The "best" country in the world is none other than the United States of America. Moreover, if you press further with your inquiries you will discover that people think that free enterprise, free elections, and freedom of worship are necessary if the good life is to be secured for individuals in any part of the world. These opinions may spring from the worthiest of motives, but they are not philosophical judgments—not that one expected to find many philosophers in the second ward.

Political philosophy must rise above national ideology, indeed above all ideology. Americans who think America is the best country going should be obliged to demonstrate that they have studied all the other countries of the world, and have found them inferior to America after measuring them by some philosophic standard. For generalizations about how men and governments ought to behave should be framed in terms of enduring principles. This, for example, is what St. Thomas Aquinas had in mind when he spoke of the existence of a Natural Law. This body of precepts prescribes proper behavior at all times and in all places. But it is not a rigid doctrine, nor is it based on the experience of a single country. The Natural Law, St. Thomas points out, does not necessarily affirm the right to private property. This right, he says, should only be guaranteed if the principle of individual ownership fits in harmoniously with the general pattern of life of a society. Philosophy, then, deals with principles of political conduct. The pitfall to be avoided is that of attempting to defend one's own personal or national interests on philosophic grounds. To do that is to elevate personal opinions to an unwarranted height; it is, indeed, to indulge in ideology. Political philosophy, like political science, demands a detached and objective attitude of mind. None of us can be completely objective, but it is a goal we must strive for as best we can.

POLITICAL INSTITUTIONS

Most students of politics, most of the time, study the actual operations of governments. Scientific methods may be used in such study, and philosophical principles may underlie evaluations and analysis. But the central focus of politics is on the workings of contemporary institutions.

What is an "institution"? Very simply, it is a group of people working toward a common aim. Thus a political party, a judicial tribunal, a legislative body, an administrative bureau—all these are institutions. The people who comprise them may come and go as time passes. Thus, the leaders of the Republican party will rise and fall over a period of years but the party continues as an institution. Moreover, the common aim that an institution pursues can be a very general one. The members of Congress, for example, will not always agree on which bills should be passed or in what form. Nor will the judges of the Supreme Court always hand down unanimous decisions. But they do agree on when to meet, on how to handle their business, and on what it is they are supposed to be doing. Thus all congressmen know they are in Washington to pass laws; all justices know it is their job to decide cases. An institution, then, consists of individuals, general goals, and rules for reaching those goals. There can be a one-man institution such as the Presidency; or a multimillion-member institution such as a political party. Some institutions have limited goals and others have more comprehensive programs. In some the members are strong in their loyalty to the group's aims; in others they are apathetic or even obstructive. It remains to say that politics cannot function without institutions, and an understanding of politics requires an awareness of how they operate.

HOW GOVERNMENT OPERATES   The student of institutions wants to find out how men organize themselves to secure ends they think desirable. In the context of American government such an undertaking might inquire:

How are individual freedoms guaranteed?
Where does the sovereign power reside?
How do citizens select their rulers?
Who makes the laws?
How are laws administered and enforced?
What is the proper role of government?

These questions, needless to say, are highly theoretical; and any attempt to discuss them in generalized terms will probably end in frustration. What is needed is an understanding of specific institutions and their operation. Some of these institutions might be:

The writ of certiorari
The Tenth Amendment to the Constitution
Party primaries and nominating conventions
The Rules Committee of the House of Representatives
The Bureau of the Budget
The Tennessee Valley Authority

Thus, the Supreme Court plays a vital role in deciding which liberties are to be guaranteed to citizens. The Court will hear a case if four justices indicate, through a writ of certiorari, that they think such a hearing is warranted. The writ itself may be no more than a rule on a piece of paper, but it is the Supreme Court acting as an institution that uses the rule to protect the freedoms of individuals. By the same token the Court employs the Tenth Amendment, another rule on paper, to decide which are the sovereign powers of the several states and which powers belong properly to the Federal government. Thus, freedoms are defined and sovereignty is located through institutional means. Meaningful answers to theoretical questions are given in the decisions of our highest judicial institution.

If it is asked how citizens select the men and women who are to hold public office, a large part of the answer lies in the process whereby candidates are nominated. Hence, it is necessary to know who participates in the primaries and who attends the nominating conventions—and how these institutions work. Moreover, some study must be given to the reasons why people participate in party politics and why they vote as they do. Where, for example, do citizens get their political values? How do they express their values through voting? Quite clearly such study must be "scientific" in the sense that the behavior of voters must be examined in a systematic way.

While it is obvious that our elected lawmakers make our laws, it is also true that in the Congress there are centers of power having disproportionate control over the legislative process. Here an institution like the Rules Committee of the House of Representatives will play a crucial role. For despite the fact that all congressmen have one vote, there is nevertheless a complex network of agencies within the Congress deciding which issues will ultimately become law of the land.

The executive power is vested in the President, but the Constitution spells out this power in only the most rudimentary way. If he has the responsibility of administering and enforcing the laws, he must find institutional means for doing the job at hand. Over the years, therefore, the Presidency has evolved methods for coordinating the activities of its administration. An important institution is the Bureau of the Budget, a body reporting directly to the White House and one that helps the President to control the multifarious functions of the executive branch. While presidential power depends in large measure on the temperament of the Chief Executive and the temper of the times, its day-to-day operations rely heavily on institutions like the Bureau of the Budget.

To ask what is the proper role of government in American society is to pose a philosophical question. But before one starts developing one's own ideas on the matter it is worth giving some attention to the functions that government currently performs. The Tennessee Valley Authority, for example, is an institution owned and operated by the Federal government; and, among other things, it is in the business of producing and selling electric power. Why is the government in this business at all? How efficient is the TVA operation? Before commencing on philosophical speculation it is advisable to examine the institutions upon which judgment is to be passed.

HOW TO STUDY A POLITICAL PROBLEM   Government is a highly complex operation, and patterns of political behavior are highly variable. On some occasions it is possible to generalize, on others it is not and one must settle for an understanding of how different institutions operate in their own setting. For example, sometimes it is appropriate to make a general statement about the workings of all American legislative chambers. But on certain matters it is necessary to distinguish between the Senate, the House of Representatives, and the state legislatures. A good rule of thumb is that whenever possible one should work from the particular to the general, drawing detailed information together and framing conclusions of ever-widening applicability.

If the goal of political study is the creation of valid generalizations, the path to this goal is not as smooth as might first appear. Ideological overtones are apt to infuse any attempt at either "scientific" or "philosophical" conclusions, and these intrusions must be guarded against. The student must seek an awareness of his personal values and must sense when they are prejudicing his analysis. He must also be willing to compare his findings and conclusions with those of others, for only out of such a community of knowledge does the whole truth emerge. If facts are to be used to support a conclusion, then they must be gathered and organized according to a system: the method of inquiry must be easily described and made available to anyone who wishes to duplicate one's research so as to test its validity. Finally, there are considerations of values in all of political study and these values lie at the foundation of political life. There is no significance in simply describing an institution of government as an end in itself. Citizens engage in politics to achieve purposes they think right, and by the same token the student must frame his researches in a philosophical context. He, too, must ask what are the aims and ends of governmental activity. And he must be prepared to evaluate that activity on the basis of principles which he has not only selected for himself but which he must be able to defend.

The study of politics, then, consists of weaving together a cloth of many fabrics. Political science and political philosophy must be synthesized in a coherent way; political institutions and political behavior must be viewed in a framework of interaction; political ideology and political principle must be described and differentiated. The final arrangement of these various approaches is the task of each person who elects to observe and comment upon the political scene. For it is his imagination, coupled with his intelligence and his powers of perception, that must make ultimate sense out of that omnipresent phenomenon we call the political life.

Review Questions

1. Does democracy postulate that all political opinions are equal?

2. What is ideology?

3. How does political science differ from the natural and physical sciences? In what ways is it similar?

4. Why do students of politics find value in Plato's *Republic?*

5. How does a political philosophy differ from a personal opinion?

6. What is an institution?

CE

MAN AND SOCIETY

Chapter 2

The drama of politics is played on the stage we call society. And its cast of characters consists of men and women of varying backgrounds, interests, and temperaments. Political life can only be understood if it is related to its social setting and viewed in terms of the human beings who give it form. Theories of politics, therefore, must be underpinned by theories of man and society.

HUMAN NATURE

The question—What is Man?—has been asked for thousands of years and has yet to receive a satisfactory answer. Neither professional philosophers nor amateur observers can agree on the essential characteristics of human nature. Although everyone has had experience of life among his fellow men, each person has a different perception of himself and those around him. In consequence, a whole multitude of theories have developed, no one of which is wholly true and none which can be proven to be altogether false. But it is possible to stand aside and analyze these contrasting perceptions of man. And in the course of doing so it may be concluded that the truth lies somewhat closer to one view than to another.

GOOD OR EVIL? "That men are actually wicked, a sad and continued experience of them proves beyond doubt," one theorist writes. "But, all the same, I think I have shown that man is naturally good."[1] According to this view all men are born into the world in a state of natural goodness. They are benign creatures, endowed with the potentiality for harmonious life with their fellows. Thus the traits of altruism, congeniality, and compassion are seen as being innate in the human species. If men and women are regarded as isolated individuals there is much evidence to support the theory of natural goodness. Apart from occasional misanthropes it is clear that human beings are capable of expressing kindness and generosity. Even those who appear to be cynical and callous in their dealings with others can be shown to have a warmer side to their nature. The heart of gold beneath the jaded exterior is, of course, a cliché of countless movie scripts, television programs, and magazine stories. It is interesting to note how audiences of millions accept the proposition of man's essential goodness. More interesting perhaps is the fact that we *want* to believe that man is good.

But the modern world is no paradise. Indeed, since the beginning of history societies and nations have been blemished by war, injustice, and tyranny. If man is naturally good, then how can these evils be explained? The usual response is to begin by assuming that man himself possesses and has always possessed the ability to live in peace and freedom. When men act perversely it is because they have been corrupted by the institutions of society. For no theory proposes that "society" is naturally good. There are all kinds of societies and social institutions, some of which bring out the best in man and others that degrade him. Thus, if men exhibit selfish behavior it is because they live in a society that compels or rewards such attributes. Some writers claim that the institution of private property makes men materialistic and causes them

[1] Jean-Jacques Rousseau, *A Discourse on the Origin of Inequality*, in *The Social Contract and Discourses* (translated by G. D. H. Cole), J. M. Dent & Sons, Ltd., Publishers, London, 1913, p. 222.

to promote their own interests to the detriment of others. Different thinkers feel that the expansion of governmental power prevents individuals from developing their true capabilities. But in both cases the men and women who make up society are not to be blamed for acting as they do. The responsibility must be attributed to the rise of certain institutions, institutions that cramp and corrupt the natural goodness that is waiting to be released if only given the chance.

ORIGINAL SIN "History," another theorist asserts, "consists for the greater part of the miseries brought upon the world by pride, ambition, avarice, revenge, lust, sedition, hypocrisy, ungoverned zeal, and all the traits of disorderly appetites which shake the public."[2] Not only is this the history of the human condition as it has been in the past; it is a description of human nature as it always will be. Pride, ambition, avarice—all these characteristics and more are, it is suggested, sewn into the nature of man. Individuals may display an altruistic side from time to time, but it is a mistake to assume that men are for that reason naturally good. On the contrary, the evidence of history is that people are usually concerned with their own welfare first and foremost. If men have the potentiality for living in peace and harmony, it is asked, then how is it that this potentiality has not been realized in the several thousand years of political life? Indeed the world's recent experience of tyranny and injustice indicates that men are as evil in our time as they have ever been in the past. Probably more so.

The doctrine of original sin postulates that human nature is unchanging and unchangeable. Since Adam's act of disobedience, this theory proceeds, all men have been tainted by his transgression. Each individual born onto this earth is a fallible creature and during his lifetime he will act in perverse ways. All men without exception exhibit these failings, and all societies everywhere inevitably contain at least a few dissentient members who undermine efforts to create social harmony. According to this view, institutions are not the molders of character but rather reflections of human nature. If there are inequalities of wealth or power, these stem from the self-interest that is built into social behavior. Any attempt to reform the basic structure of society, moreover, will be as unsuccessful as an attempt to alter human character. This is because both societies and men are the products of a history they did not themselves make. And even such social and politi-

[2] Edmund Burke, *Reflections on the Revolution in France*, J. M. Dent & Sons, Ltd., Publishers, London, 1910, p. 137.

cal changes that are effected will seldom bring the consequences that the reformers originally intended. Human perversity cannot be abolished by plans or programs. The best that can be done is to control the worst manifestations of this perversity by means of political authority. If freedom and justice are to have any meaning then they must be underpinned by the power of government. "Society," Burke continues, "requires not only that the passions of individuals should be subjected, but that even in the mass and body, as well as in the individuals, the inclinations of men should frequently be thwarted, their will controlled, and their passions brought into subjection."[3]

RATIONAL OR IRRATIONAL? "Why is it," one writer asks, "that there is on the whole a preponderance among mankind of rational opinions and rational conduct?"[4] The answer he gives is straightforward. To begin with, if man were not rational—that is, unable to select means to achieve the ends he desires—then the business of politics and society would deteriorate into chaos. History does show that men have been able, by the use of reason, to devise ways of collecting garbage, delivering the mail, and even on occasion of preventing wars. Rationality is possible because man is a creature who has shown himself capable of learning by experience. His knowledge is cumulative and he can forebear from repeating the mistakes of the past. This, at least, is one view of human nature. The question of whether man is fundamentally rational or irrational is different from but related to the question of whether he is basically good or evil. Men can be good but also irrational; they can be evil but nevertheless rational. One question deals with the shape of the human spirit; the other with the powers of the human mind.

It can be argued that just as men are good when approached as isolated individuals, so are they rational when they consider the affairs in the solitude of their own home. However, once men are brought together in crowds they tend to lose their heads. They can be stirred by demagogues and lured into supporting policies and programs that they would reject in a saner moment. Thus apparently rational individuals will become transformed as they join a lynch mob or a revolutionary movement. So will hitherto prudent citizens vote for programs without providing the money to pay for them or the personnel to

[3] *Ibid.*, p. 57.
[4] John Stuart Mill, *On Liberty*, in *Utilitarianism, Liberty, and Representative Government*, J. M. Dent & Sons, Ltd., Publishers, London, 1910, p. 80.

implement them. The conclusion emerges that if men as individuals are rational, society as an entity is often lacking this quality.

Juxtaposed against this view is an altogether different theory. Here it is proposed that men are irrational, that they are creatures of passion and interest. "Thus the passions of men are gratified," another writer says. "They develop themselves and their aims in accordance with their natural tendencies, and build up the edifice of human society. . . . In history an additional result is commonly produced by human actions beyond that which they aim at and obtain."[5] The thought is that history has a rationality of its own, a logic that unfolds independent of the behavior of individuals. Thus, as thousands or millions of men and women strive to gratify their passions or promote their interests, there come into being consequences that they did not anticipate and which they cannot prevent. The course of history, then, is unrelenting and is guided by a reason of its own. The best that men can hope for is to *understand* the underlying forces that move nations and societies. According to this view, knowledge rather than action should be the goal. For at least it can be said that men who understand the reason of history will not be surprised or bewildered as the future unfolds around them.

ORDINARY MEN AND EXTRAORDINARY MEN Is it possible to generalize about human nature? For it is plain that men and women possess different qualities and temperaments, and it is hard to put down the suspicion that some people are superior to others. There are two questions to be answered here. The first is whether there actually are "superior" individuals in society. The second is that, granting that there are such people, of finding or identifying them. Some theorists believe so strongly in the doctrine of human equality that they minimize the differences among people. While admitting that men vary in physical strength, intellect, or ambition they insist that the qualities all men share are more significant than those that separate them. The equalitarian theory will be discussed in some detail later on. Now is the time to consider the notion that societies may be differentiated into common men, on the one hand, and uncommon men, on the other.

There are several ways to differentiating the ordinary individuals in a population from those who are endowed with extraordinary qualities. These usually concern one "aristocracy" or another, a select group

[5] Georg Wilhelm Friedrich Hegel, *Philosophy of History* (translated by J. Sibree), Dover Publications, Inc., New York, 1956, p. 27.

whose members are presumably superior to the run-of-the-mill citizens in whose midst they exist. Three kinds of aristocracies may be distinguished:

1. The first may be called an "aristocracy of breeding." This consists of men and women who possess inherited wealth, privileged education, and who are members of families that have exercised power and responsibility for at least several generations. What makes these people superior? The argument is sometimes made that "blood tells," that genetic inheritance produces superior qualities in certain family lines. However, this theory is questionable, if only because even the best families have their share of idiots and immoralists. Rather the argument rests on the fact that those who are brought up in an atmosphere of inherited wealth develop a sense of security and self-confidence that is usually denied to others. This aristocracy has both the education and the leisure to evolve a style of life that raises the level of culture and civility in society. Having roots in their national tradition and being able to take a long-range perspective on the future, their approach to politics is conservative in the best sense. And because members of this aristocracy have material security they enter civic or political life out of a sense of duty. This means they can promote the broader interests of society and do not have to pander to the momentary whims of a capricious electorate. A man of wealth does not have to build a political career in order to feed his family. He can be available when he is needed; but he can also resign when he feels his principles are being compromised. To be sure, not all individuals in this class display this sense of responsibility. There is no shortage of playboys among the old rich. But what is argued is that an aristocracy of breeding does, on the whole, promote the higher values and the finer things of life. Although this aristocracy may live well off the sweat of others, the culture that it sustains raises the quality of life for everyone. Whether it be art or literature or constitutional liberty, the suggestion is that these values are supported by a minority of wealth, education, and leisure. And all of society profits because such standards are strengthened and transmitted.

2. The members of an "aristocracy of intellect" may have their origins in any of the classes of society. High intelligence is not the exclusive property of any single group, and rational individuals are distributed at random up and down the social scale. Of course, a person from a wealthy background stands a better chance of having his intellectual potentialities developed. For he will receive encouragement from his

parents and the benefits of higher education. However, experience has shown that many of our finest intellects have sprung from humble surroundings and many of them have all but educated themselves. What is being proposed is that there are some people who possess extraordinary minds. These individuals have powers of perception usually denied to others. They can see an order in human affairs and they can discern major trends that are obscure to the generality of their fellow citizens. Most members of this aristocracy have little contact with the business of politics; they are writers or teachers or are similarly removed from the circles where power is exercised. However, some theorists have suggested that the good society will only be attained when philosophers are made kings or kings are turned into philosophers. These proposals are made because throughout history there has been a wide gulf between power and reason. Seldom are men of superior intellect placed in positions where they may have an influence on the conduct of government. That such an aristocracy exists is seldom questioned even though its members cannot be identified by family background or inherited wealth. The important question is whether these people should play a greater role in politics, especially at the higher reaches where policies of far-reaching implications are made.

It is sometimes suggested that among the aristocracy of intellect there are persons of superior *moral* knowledge. Here are individuals who can rise above emotions and interests, and who can see the meaning of justice and virtue in ways that others cannot. Such men of reason can detect the common good or the general welfare while others think only of self-interest. In this sense rationality means not only being able to perceive the world as it is but also being able to judge how the world ought to be. The argument therefore is that wisdom must be joined by virtue, that the select group of citizens who possess these qualities should be elevated to positions of power and influence. To be sure, there is bound to be controversy over what is virtue or what is the common good. But few will deny that it is better to have men of moral sensibility in government than men who think only of power and profit.

3. One of the reasons why the aristocracies of breeding and intellect are not as prominent as they might be in political life is that they are often overshadowed by another group. For there is an "aristocracy of talent" in every society and its members invariably ascend to positions of power. The aptitude for exercising power, for inducing others to act as one wishes them to, belongs to only a minority of citizens. It is

often found in those of privileged background, for they have the self-confidence that gives the authority to command. It is sometimes found in those of superior intellect because they can discern the symbols and techniques that make men obey. But on the whole the talents of power are randomly distributed among the classes of a population, and very frequently these talents bear little relation to family background or high intelligence. At the head of armies and of mobs, of business enterprises and government bureaucracies, indeed in all situations where men work and act together, will be found talented individuals who know how to lead others.

Such extraordinary individuals may spend little time considering questions of culture or morality. They are more expert in manipulating means than they are in pondering ends. Many of them have devoted time and energy to building their careers and they think more of their own prospects than they do of the common good. Moreover, the talents of leadership are governed by the time, the place, and the circumstances. A man may show great abilities for leading a revolutionary movement and if he is available at the right juncture he will be able to exercise his superior talents. However, another epoch in history may call for someone to oversee a complex bureaucracy, and here will be needed an individual who can administer intricate policies and lead an organization. In other words, the talent for haranguing a mob is quite different from the talent of heading a civil service. Yet both are talents and both are talents of leadership. Whether men with either of these aptitudes may properly be called an "aristocracy" is often disputed. For the ability to lead leaves open the question of the goals that are being pursued. Quite clearly, most successful leaders are not philosophers and many promote the interests of a group or a class rather than that of society as a whole. But talent cannot be submerged for long, and men able to exercise power will always find an outlet for their calling.

Any theory of human nature, therefore, must take account of the characteristics that differentiate individuals from each other. Men may be good or evil or a mixture of the two. They may be rational or irrational or both. But there is always the suspicion that there are some people who are exceptions to any generalizations about human nature. Whether it is legitimate to talk of such persons as extraordinary is a recurrent question of political theory. It may be that superior breeding or intellect or talent sets particular individuals apart from the rest of their fellow men and women. Or it may be that despite their superiority in some respects they are, in essentials, pretty much like the rest of us.

THE STRUCTURE OF SOCIETY

Theories of society can either attempt to describe the structure of society as it actually is or they can propose ways in which it should be organized. However, this simple distinction between "scientific" theories on the one hand, and "philosophical" theories on the other, is seldom manifested in political writings. What usually happens is that a theorist begins with his own conception of the *good* society. It may well be that he prefers arrangements pretty much as they are. If this is the case, then his "scientific" description of reality will actually highlight the more pleasing aspects of the *status quo* and will tend to overlook those which are more depressing. Another theorist may be upset with things as they are, and for him the good society will be radically different from what he sees about him. In this instance, his "scientific" description will emphasize the unsavory conditions of the present system. This needs to be said because every theory of society is necessarily colored by the moral preconceptions of its author. The observer, in the final analysis, sees the society he *wants* to see. The value of a theory lies in its ability to convince others that its depiction of reality is consistent with their own experience of life in this world. It is not surprising, therefore, that there are two quite different and opposing views of society in political theory. These may be called the "atomistic" view and the "organic" view.

THE ATOMISTIC VIEW   "The community is a fictitious body," one theorist writes, "composed of the individual persons who are considered as constituting as it were its members."[6] When someone calls community or society a "fiction" his intention is to stress the fact that these entities are no more than collections of individual citizens. This atomistic view asserts that any social whole is simply the sum of its individual parts. To claim that a community or a society is somehow greater than or independent of the people who compose it is a risky enterprise. For then one is tempted to say that society has a "life" or a "purpose" or

[6] Jeremy Bentham, *The Principles of Morals and Legislation,* in Wilfrid Harrison (ed.), *A Fragment on Government and the Principles of Morals and Legislation,* Basil Blackwell & Mott, Ltd., Oxford, 1948, p. 129.

even a "destiny" of its own, and such an assertion is pure conjecture. At all events, the atomistic approach assumes that a society and its component institutions is brought into being by men for reasons of necessity or convenience. A number of theorists have argued, for example, that at some time in the past citizens came out of the primeval forest ("the state of nature") and formally agreed to set up society and government ("the social contract") as a means of solving the problems of anarchy and injustice. Although the ideas of a "state of nature" and a "social contract" are themselves fictions, they serve to emphasize the point that society exists for the benefit of its citizens.

This also means that social and political institutions—churches, schools, businesses, associations, courts, legislatures—must give evidence that they exist to further the welfare of the people who either belong to them or who must submit to their authority. The atomistic theory implies that there should be a minimum of barriers to the development of individual potentialities. Society must serve the needs of citizens and encourage them to evolve their best qualities. For this reason social and political power should be fragmented rather than concentrated. Whether the power of government or any other institution is being considered, the suspicion remains that any concentration of power deters individuals from expressing themselves to the foremost of their capabilities. For government and society are a fabric of regulations and rules, and a surfeit of restrictions dampen the human spirit and destroy initiative. It is not surprising, therefore, that the atomistic view often postulates an elemental conflict between "man and the state" or between "authority and the individual." Such tensions do indeed exist, and the atomistic prescription is that they should be resolved in favor of the citizen rather than the state or society. The answer is less clear-cut, of course, when there are conflicts between citizen and citizen. And there are also cases of discord between a majority of citizens on the one hand and a minority on the other. Both majority and minority are collections of individuals, and principles must be devised for settling the differences of opinion and interest that inevitably occur.

ATOMISM AND PLURALISM   No society is an undifferentiated mass of autonomous individuals. Every society has a "structure," and in the atomistic view this structure is a network of groups and associations. People in a society may be distinguished from each other on the basis of race or religion or national origin. They will live in different regions of the country and hence have different habits and patterns of thought. Thus there will be Protestants and Roman Catholics, Italian-Americans and Anglo-Saxons, New Yorkers and Californians, and so forth. Some of these group memberships or identifications will change as individuals shift their residence or are assimilated into new strata of the society. What is being stressed, however, is that there is a diversity of groups and that these groups interact with each other in much the same way that individuals do among themselves. At the same time citizens are free to identify with one or another group so long as such identification proves advantageous to them. There is nothing in the atomistic theory that says that a person must remain a Presbyterian or a Pennsylvanian if he finds such a role constricting. To be sure, a person cannot throw off his racial background. But he can, if he works at it, go a long way toward severing his ties with a group that ceases to give him the opportunities he wants.

By the same token an atomistic society is a "nation of joiners." There are many associations ranging from garden clubs to political parties, from civic welfare organizations to lobbies and pressure groups. The assumption is that people join these associations voluntarily with a variety of motives. It is further supposed that most people are "joiners" and are prepared to promote their interests by combining with others who have similar views. The motive may be simply to have fun: such as forming a ski club or a bowling league. Or it may be economic and political: such as joining together to petition the legislature to pass a certain law that will benefit a business or an industry. The fact that society contains many associations has a number of consequences. For one thing, it takes individuals out of a state of isolation and gives them a chance to participate with others in a common endeavor. For another, it permits citizens to have a variety of loyalties and allegiances, thus preventing the possibility that they might live under a single source of authority. Finally, a network of voluntary associations stands as a "buffer" between the relatively powerless individual and the potentially powerful state. In a way association membership can act as a "shield" that protects a person from victimization at the hands of the agencies of government. Pluralism, therefore, is a natural accompaniment of the atomistic views of society and human freedom. The atomistic society, far from consisting of a mass of isolated individuals, is actually a web of associations and groups that link men and women with each other.

THE ORGANIC VIEW "Because it is the completion of associations existing by nature," another theorist writes, "every *polis* [i.e., society] exists by nature, having itself the same quality as the earlier associations from which it grew."[7] This conception looks on society as a natural phenomenon, having grown out of the family, the clan, and more primitive forms of collective life. To regard society as an "organism" is to see it as a series of fixed relationships between people and institutions. That is, each citizen and association has a particular place and function in the social whole, and it is the obligation of each to contribute to the life and purpose of the community. Thus society at any point in time is the most recent culmination of a long natural and historical development. Rather than being a contract of convenience made by men and capable of being broken by them, it is a living organism with a past and a future. Moreover, in the organic view a society is a genuine community; citizens have a sense of belonging and they receive their values and their identity from participation in communal life.

This society is also pluralistic, but it is a different kind of pluralism. There will be a variety of groups and associations; however, they will not move around aimlessly like so many atoms. On the contrary, churches and civic organizations and fraternal groups will have a fairly fixed location in the social structure, locations established by history and tradition. Indeed, the entire structure of the organic society is characterized by a hierarchy. There will be various classes of citizens existing in a pyramidal order and each class will have its own rights and responsibilities. Thus, while the members of the upper class may have inherited wealth and power, they will also assume the duty of acting in the best interests of those arrayed beneath them in the social order. Out of this arrangement there emerges a dependence of all groups and classes upon one another. For the rich need the poor just as the poor need the rich. The relationship is not one of exploitation, but rather of mutual acknowledgment that each part of the community has a role to play in the pursuit of the common good.

COMMUNITY AND INDIVIDUALITY The organic society cannot permit too much mobility on the part of individuals. For the happiness of the citizens and the welfare of the community, it is best that each person remain throughout his life in the region and class in which he was born. For individuals can maintain a meaningful set of values and

[7] Aristotle, *Politics* (translated by Ernest Barker), Oxford University Press, Fair Lawn, N. J., 1946, p. 4.

society will remain stable only if everyone accepts his traditional role and carries it out to the best of his ability. Even the most humble of occupations has a dignity of its own, and the rubrics of "success" and "failure" have no meaning in an organic setting. Each citizen, and not simply those at the summit of the social pyramid, profits from remaining in his established station. For by doing so he finds human relationships predictable and he can be sure that the values of his forebears are applicable to life as he knows it. While the atomistic theory stresses individualism, its organic counterpart underlines the security and contentment produced by living in a community where each citizen is respected for the part he takes in promoting the welfare of all. Individual happiness, then, stands in an integral relationship to the stability and health of the entire society. Progress is a slow historical process and the institutions of social life are the results of a natural evolution. Attempts to hasten or upset this development by artificial means will end in chaos, for the fabric of an organic society is woven in a complex pattern that is easily torn but virtually impossible to repair.

ATOMISTIC OR ORGANIC? Two standard questions must be asked in the course of evaluating any theory. The first is: Does the theory give a satisfactory description of social and political life as it actually *is*? The second is: Does it provide a persuasive prescription for the kind of society and political system that *ought* to exist? Both of these questions are relevant to the atomistic and organic theories; for both deal with description and prescription, with the "is" and the "ought."

Most commentators will agree that, in general outlines, modern societies are more atomistic than organic. They argue that industrialization and urbanization have liberated individuals from the fixed roles and relationships of an earlier time. The organic theory may have been an adequate description of agrarian society of the feudal or preindustrial epoch. Institutions today take on more of the fluid character of voluntary associations than they do the established patterns of medieval guilds. The organic theorist does not deny the fact of industrialization, nor does he ignore the fact that mobility has become accelerated in recent generations. What he does say is that despite these developments society remains the essential organism that it always was. Many modern trends, such as the rapid growth of industry and cities and the displacement of individuals from the classes and callings in which they were reared, are actually harmful to the proper functioning of the organism. Society, in a word, has been growing too rapidly for its own good. Moreover, its movements have been in the wrong direction, for they tend to deprive men of the moral values and sense of security that they need to lead the full life.

Thus the question becomes a moral one. The defender of the atomistic view claims that his kind of society liberates men, that it releases them from feudal bonds and allows them to develop their full potentialities as individuals. The proponent of the organic view counters that there is such a thing as having too much freedom, that individuals can only lead the good life if they receive from society an established position and an authoritative set of values. In a sense, the question revolves around how much freedom men want or need, and how this freedom is to be defined. It is also a question concerning the definition of human nature, for until one has a clear conception of man's capabilities it is impossible to know what kind of society he must have if he is to experience freedom and happiness.

Review Questions

1. What does it mean to say that "man is naturally good"?

2. In what senses can some men be said to be superior to others?

3. What is a "social contract"?

4. What is pluralism?

5. How can society be an organism?

6. Is progress always desirable?

ENDS AND MEANS

Chapter 3

The great issues of political theory have been defined and debated for 2,000 years. The vocabulary of political theory, unlike that of many other disciplines, is a part of the public domain. Thus, everyone is prepared to discourse on liberty and equality, on law and justice, on power and policy. Indeed, there are many people who feel that they have their own "theories" on these subjects. But not all attempts to generalize about political life are worthy of being called theoretical. A theory must be clear and consistent, it must be grounded on a sophisticated awareness of the facts, it must not be distorted by emotions or interests. This does not mean that two theories cannot reach opposed conclusions. Indeed, this is just what occurred in the case of theories about society. Probably the best way to discuss this question is to turn to some actual theories dealing with significant political issues.

TWO THEORIES OF FREEDOM

FREEDOM FROM RESTRAINT   "By liberty, is understood, according to the proper signification of the word, the absence of external impediments," one theorist writes.[1] A free man, according to this theory, is one who is not prevented from doing the things he wants to do. Men seek to express themselves in a wide variety of ways. Some put a high premium on practicing their religion and worshiping God as their conscience dictates. Others like to make speeches or write books. Still others desire to form political parties or social movements. And yet another group wishes to run their own businesses and enrich themselves in the process. To be able to do these things is to be free. To want to do them but to be barred from doing so is to be subjected to oppression. The quest for freedom, then, involves removing the barriers to individual action. It also involves preventing the raising of new barriers. The old dictum is also a true one: Eternal vigilance is the price of liberty. The problem for some men is keeping the freedoms they have. The problem for others is securing the freedoms they want but do not have. Needless to say, in many instances a victory on the part of the "have-nots" may result in a diminution of the freedoms of the "haves."

FREEDOM AND GOVERNMENT   What are the barriers to individual freedom? Some theorists regard the government as the foremost threat to individual liberty. There is more than enough evidence in history to show that governments have proscribed religions, banned books and speeches, abolished parties, and confiscated property. It is not surprising that governments have been able to do this, for the state has at its disposal the power to make and enforce laws and it has in its service the police and the army. A free society, in this view, is one in which the powers of government are severely limited in scope. The customary proposal is that the functions of government be outlined in a constitution, which specifies what kind of laws are permitted and what kind are prohibited. In this way citizens have a defined area of freedom, where they may express themselves without suffering from government regulation or interference.

[1] Thomas Hobbes, *Leviathan*, Michael Oakeshott (ed.), Basil Blackwell & Mott, Ltd., Oxford, 1946, p. 84.

While government has both the power to make laws and the power to coerce citizens, many writers and thinkers see that impediments to freedom can spring from other sources in society. It is often argued that individuals are frustrated in their desires not by the state but by other of their fellow citizens. Neighbors may make life difficult for someone who tries to practice an unconventional religion. A wealthy and powerful employer may, in various ways, deprive his employees of freedoms they think they should have. Now it may be that in either or both of these cases the government supports the dominant religion or the dominant economic class. But this is not always so. And if it is not the case, then the religious heretics and the exploited employees may look to the government for protection. In other words, they hope that the use of governmental power against one section of the community will permit them the freedoms they did not previously have. According to this analysis, the government can be the guarantor of freedoms. The big question, therefore, is which class or group in society can either dominate the governmental machinery or at least gain access to it. Nevertheless, whether the state is regarded as the enemy or friend of liberty the overarching view here is that freedom is something that the individual can define and evaluate for himself. The idea is that each citizen knows what it is he wants to do and he can tell whether or not he is being allowed to do it.

POSITIVE FREEDOM ". . . He will be forced to be free," another theorist writes, "for this is the condition which, by giving each citizen to his country, secures him against all personal dependence."[2] How can someone be "forced" to be free? By commonsense standards, freedom and compulsion are contradictory terms. The answer is that genuine freedom consists in doing not simply what one wants to do but in doing what one *ought* to do. Many human wants are little more than momentary whims. Gratifying these urges is a kind of freedom, but it certainly is not a very elevated form. Everyone at one time or another acts "against his better judgment." However, that moment of reflection often comes too late in the day or even too late in life. For some people it never comes at all. Therefore if people are to be truly free they must actually be prevented from doing some of the things they want to do—or think they want to do. What is implied in this view, furthermore, is that society rather than the individual has the best understanding of what constitutes the free life. The history of one's

[2] Jean-Jacques Rousseau, *Social Contract*, in *op. cit.*, p. 15.

nation and the customs of one's community have evolved values and standards by which freedom is defined. If a person is thrown on his own resources and tries to find a meaningful definition of freedom by himself, the odds are that he will fail in this endeavor. He is, in the final analysis, a citizen of his country and a member of his community, and true freedom for him is ultimately to be found in accepting the morality that has been prepared for him.

This, then, is why some dissentient citizens must be "forced" to be free. Put simply, they may think they know what conditions they *want* in order to be free; but they are actually ignorant of the conditions they *need* to be truly free. Furthermore, once they have been compelled to take an opposite or alternative path, they will usually acknowledge that they had been wrong in their earlier judgment. The positive theory of freedom, therefore, is concerned with raising men to the level where they can best exercise whatever mental and moral faculties they have. The emphasis, in sum, is on being free to do the things one ought to be doing. And it is the responsibility of government to educate and elevate citizens in this positive direction.

The positive theory would appear to be saying that the average person is incapable of knowing his own best interests. Does this mean that every society must have, and every government should be headed by, an elite that defines the meaning of freedom for everyone else? Some writers do suggest that rule by philosopher-kings is the only solution for the problem of freedom. However, most of them assume that the essential spirit of freedom is not to be handed down by an elite but is rather to be found in the history, the customs, and the traditions of a nation or a community. This means that attention must be paid both to the past and to the consensus that characterizes the present. Freedom is best viewed as the composite of freedoms that a society already possesses and the utility of which has been proven by time and experience. Does this mean, too, that the positive theory of freedom is fundamentally conservative? It is certainly true that it frequently accompanies the organic view of society and is used as an argument against social or political reform. But others than conservatives have taken the positive and organic approach. Two theorists, hardly notable for their fondness of the *status quo*, write, "Only in community with others has each individual the means of cultivating his gifts in all directions; only in the community, therefore, is personal freedom possible."[3] In other words, positive freedom can be a revolutionary

[3] Karl Marx and Friedrich Engels, *German Ideology*, International Publishers Company, Inc., New York, 1947, p. 74.

as well as a conservative theory. For both revolutionaries and conservatives are critical of the view of man and society that permits atomistic individuals to clash and compete with each other in their selfish drive for wealth, status, and power.

FREEDOM OF THE WILL "The authority of a king is physical and controls the actions of men without subduing their will," a theorist writes. "But the majority possesses a power that is physical and moral at the same time, which acts upon the will as much as upon the actions."[4] A tyrannical ruler may ban all opposition parties and jail or threaten with imprisonment those who criticize his regime. These restraints on expression are oppressive to those who suffer them, but at least the use of power in this instance is visible to the eye. A man who has been imprisoned by a tyrant sees and feels his chains. But his mind remains free; he is being oppressed and he *knows* he is being oppressed. However, there are other and more subtle forms of tyranny. A country may ostensibly be a democracy, where the majority has the power to rule. The individuals who comprise this majority may *think* they have power, may *think* they are free, and may *think* they have formed their ideas and opinions by themselves. Yet despite this apparently happy state of affairs, the fact may be that these citizens have had their attitudes and behavior shaped for them by the pressures to conformity exerted on them by society. Thus, freedom can be endangered by a tyranny that is invisible: the power over the mind that the group exercises over its members. There are no prisons or chains but rather the internalized controls that each person accepts and even welcomes. The curious question then arises: Can a man who thinks he is free actually be a slave? Put another way: Can we distinguish the "feeling of freedom" from "genuine freedom"? If such a distinction is valid then it is necessary to give close attention to the forces that shape the minds of men. It is one thing to revolt against a visible tyrant. It is far more difficult to rebel against social pressures that cannot be felt.

EQUAL RIGHTS FOR EQUAL MEN

The discussion of theories of human nature brought out the fact that there are great differences in backgrounds and characteristics among the citizens of any society. Some are cleverer and some are more cultured. Some are more suited to the pursuit of the moral and the intel-

[4] Alexis de Tocqueville, *Democracy in America* (translated by Henry Reeve), Phillips Bradley (ed.), Vintage Books, Random House, Inc., New York, 1956, vol. I, p. 273.

lectual life. And some have greater aptitudes for exercising power or gaining wealth. No one with eyes in his head can or will deny the existence of these human differences. But what is argued is that the basic similarities among human beings outweigh and are more significant than the differences that separate them. "As to the strength of body, the weakest has strength enough to kill the strongest, either by secret machination, or by confederacy with others . . . " one theorist writes, "and as to faculties of the mind, . . . I find yet a greater equality amongst men, than that of strength."[5] In addition to physical and mental similarities it has been pointed out that men share the same basic needs. All people need to give and receive love and affection; all people need the respect of others and the feeling that they are performing a useful function in society. To be sure, it may be argued that some people will be satisfied with humbler occupations and will welcome the chance to conform to authority. Yet such a view must not be carried too far. No person wants to be the slave of another; indeed, no man wants to be deprived of a vote or a voice in his government if he sees that others have such privileges. All in all, the question of whether men are on the whole similar or different is a question of interpreting the observable facts. There may be no agreement on what the facts mean or which are the most important facts. Nevertheless, the debate can only be carried on by constant recourse to the past and present experience of man in society.

EQUALITY AND INEQUALITY "The metaphysical and alchemical legislators," another theorist writes, " . . . have attempted to confound all sorts of citizens, as well as they could, into one homogeneous mass."[6] Attempts at artificial equalization ignore the fact that some men are "naturally" superior to others, and these fortunate individuals ought to have a preferred status in society and greater power in the conduct of government. The question of who is superior and who is inferior is resolved not by looking at the facts but by having recourse to philosophy. Such a philosophy may state that some people are the "elect" of God and therefore superior to those of their fellow men who were not so chosen. Another philosophy may postulate that the social organism, like the human organism, will have both physical and moral qualities. Thus, it follows that the population will have natural gradations, some citizens doing the manual labor and others performing the higher

[5] Thomas Hobbes, *op. cit.*, p. 80.
[6] Edmund Burke, *op. cit.*, p. 181.

callings. If society is an organism it follows that all its members cannot be equal by birth or talent. Arguments over whether all men are or are not equal are difficult to settle. For the disputants have almost invariably made up their minds beforehand, being committed to a particular philosophy. The person who believes all men are equal will usually stress the observable similarities among individuals. The person who believes they are unequal will stress the differences. However, it is important to note that the citing of facts does not prove or disprove a philosophical view. Facts can illustrate such a viewpoint and can convey its meaning in a vivid way. But there will never be enough facts to validate or verify either the philosophy of equality or the philosophy of inequality. Temperament, emotion, and personal interest cause men to espouse one view or the other.

EQUAL PEOPLE AND UNEQUAL PEOPLE   In common usage the equality–inequality juxtaposition is, of course, often confused with the similar–different method of analysis. There is also another problem that arises in ordinary discussions of equality. This involves the question of which people we mean when we say that some are or are not the "equals" of others. This has important political implications for it entails a consideration of relations between majority and minority groups in society:

CASE A	CASE B
Unequals: powerful minority	*Equals:* powerful majority
Equals: powerless majority	*Unequals:* powerless minority

In Case A when it is said that some people are "unequal" to others, it means that there is a powerful or privileged minority group that has superior qualities or positions compared with the rest of the citizens. Here it is usually the people in the majority who argue for abolishing inequality, and in this case they mean that privilege should be done away with and power should be distributed in a more equitable manner. In Case B when it is said that some people are "unequal" to others, it means that there exists a powerless or underprivileged minority group that suffers oppression or discrimination at the hands of the rest of the citizens. Here it is the people in the minority who argue for abolishing inequality. Moreover, in Case A the majority and in Case B the minority protest to those in more favored positions by asserting, in so many words, "We are as good as you are!" This is the form that outcry usually takes, and it is often infused with not a little envy and arrogance. At the same time there are often some people in the minority in Case A and in the majority in Case B who have uneasy consciences about their power and privileges. These individuals look down on those less favored than themselves saying, "You are as good as we are!" But this sentiment is often expressed in tones of compassion and charity. In short, the efforts to do away with inequality may stem from quite different groups and be spurred on by quite different motives.

THE RIGHTS OF MAN "The sum of all we drive at," one theorist writes, "is that every man enjoys the same rights that are granted to others."[7] A "right" is freedom: it is the liberty of an individual to engage in one or another kind of behavior. The right of free speech means that a person can say what he pleases without being silenced by someone else. The right of private property means that a person may own his own business and conduct it in a manner that he thinks suitable to its growth and profitability. Rights, however, are a special kind of freedom because they must be accorded to all men equally. If some people are allowed to own property and others are not, then property ownership is a *privilege* and not a right. The chief characteristic of a right, then, is its equalitarian basis. But even here theory and practice may be rather far apart. For example, the right of free speech means that all citizens can say their piece without interference by the government or other citizens. For the average person this means he can climb on the proverbial soapbox and exhort all those within earshot. However, some citizens own newspapers or magazines and it is clear that their opinions will reach many more people. The right of free speech implies that *any* citizen can go into the business of publishing a newspaper or a magazine. Yet it hardly needs to be said that the average person simply does not have the money to set up a *New York Times* or a *Saturday Evening Post*. Despite the equalitarian character of the right, there will still be some voices that will be heard more loudly and more frequently than others. By the same token, every citizen is "free" to set up his own General Motors Corporation.

THE SOURCES OF RIGHTS Where do rights come from? There are, generally speaking, two schools of thought on this question. The first was incomparably expressed in a passage familiar to everyone, "We hold

[7] John Locke, *Second Treatise of Civil Government*, in E. A. Burtt (ed.), *The English Philosophers from Bacon to Mill*, Modern Library, Random House, Inc., New York, 1939, par. 159.

these truths to be self-evident,—that all men are created equal; that they are endowed by their Creator with certain unalienable rights. . . ." This is the theory of "natural rights" and it postulates that all men are *born* with certain rights and that these rights are the gift of God or some other supernatural power. What is being suggested here is that in order to lead a full life, in order to fulfill their potentialities as human beings, citizens must be guaranteed certain freedoms. Moreover, a person possesses these "natural rights" at all times and in all places. They belong to him because he is a human individual, and they remain his even if the government or society denies him the freedoms he thinks he ought to have.

The big stumbling block for natural rights is to set up some way of determining just what they are and how they should be interpreted in varying circumstances. One may postulate that natural rights do indeed exist and that they are vested by God in every individual. But suppose that a citizen claims that he has a natural right to walk the streets with no clothes on? We can ask him who told him that this form of behavior is actually a natural right. He may reply that he has pondered the matter, in a manner befitting a rational being, and has concluded that God gave man sun and air so he might enjoy those natural blessings. He may even quote a passage or two from Scripture thus lending authority to his argument. It is very difficult to refute such a claim. Thus the suspicion arises that recourse to natural rights justifications may be little more than propaganda. There is no way of testing whether a claimed right is natural or whether it is simply a personal interest that an individual wishes to gratify. Nor can it be said that a right becomes natural in character if a majority of the people think this is the case. For the Voice of God does not necessarily emanate from the mouth of the multitude. Indeed, divine sentiments are more likely to be expressed by a single isolated heretic or a small band of righteous men. Moreover, society does not have a tribunal of rational judges, in direct communication with the Deity, who can decide which claimed rights are natural and which are not. For this reason many observers have concluded that anyone and everyone with an ax to grind is apt to invoke on his side the rhetoric of natural rights.

Hence, there has emerged the view that rights are to be found on the statute books and only there. A theorist writes, "The liberty of a subject lieth only in those things, which in regulating their actions, the sovereign hath pretermitted [i.e. not expressly forbade]. . . ."[8] This means that rights are made by men and that they have their origins

[8] Thomas Hobbes, *op. cit.*, p. 139.

in the legislative, judicial, and constitutional processes of a society. A citizen has the right to free speech if a law or a constitution grants him this right, or if he can show that there is no law or constitutional provision expressly forbidding the making of speeches. In this way new rights may be created and old rights can be amended or even abolished. Indeed, rights are gained in the same way that laws are enacted or constitutions revised. Furthermore, courts play a significant role in interpreting laws and constitutions, thus telling citizens what rights they do and do not have. This theory of rights makes the definition of individual freedom very much part of the political process. For groups, acting through courts and legislatures, will plainly try to have their interests guaranteed to them in the form of rights. Such a view may be less uplifting than the natural rights theory, but it is at least a more accurate description of how people behave.

THE ENFORCEMENT OF RIGHTS One of the continuing problems of politics is that although rights may exist in theory they are not guaranteed in practice. There can be several reasons for this. One is that the agencies of law enforcement are more concerned with administrative efficiency and order than they are with the particular rights of individuals. Or, on the other hand, such agencies may be so inefficient or understaffed or lacking in power that they are unable to guarantee the rights of citizens. On other occasions enforcement officials may be less than sympathetic to the people whose rights they are supposed to protect. What this adds up to is that rights are not self-enforcing. Finally, it is not simply government that grants or withholds rights in actual practice. Society can, by exerting pressures and sanctions, cause individuals to refrain from exercising rights that they theoretically possess. These observations on the enforcement of rights can be applied both to "natural rights" and to rights that have a basis in law.

SOVEREIGNTY AND POWER

The discussion of rights demonstrated that legal authority is not always enforced and that power must underpin what is inscribed on the statute books. Nevertheless, it is important to emphasize the role of law in politics and society. Most laws are obeyed by most citizens, and nearly everyone grants that the rule of law is vital for civilized life.

SOVEREIGNTY "The legislator in all commonwealths is the only sovereign . . ." one theorist says. "For the legislator is he that makes the law."[9] This may appear to be a truism, but it has not always been so in the past and there is no assurance that it will always be so in the future. A society can have but a single "sovereign," that is, only one institution or set of institutions can be the ultimate source of law. If there are two legislatures, one in the East and one in the West, each attempting to make laws for the entire country, then it is obvious that chaos will be the only result. Virtually all societies that have tried to become nation-states in the modern world have undergone the travails of creating a single and unified sovereign. Problems of this sort continue to plague underdeveloped countries, especially if they are seeking to create a nation out of what was previously a conglomeration of tribes and villages. For sovereignty to become established there must emerge a respect for law on the part of citizens, and this means their acknowledging that one particular authority is the source of all laws. Individuals must give up—voluntarily or under compulsion—sectional loyalties, and they must take a new and expanded view of citizenship. The theory of sovereignty is a first principle of government, therefore, for until a sovereign is established there can be no meaningful talk of freedom or equality or rights. For these values are created by law and exist only as long as law is an object of respect.

Is it possible to identify the sovereign in any state or society? That is, can one locate the "seat" of sovereignty in a definitive way? For many years such a treasure hunt was a pastime of students of politics, but interest in it has waned and probably for good reason. It may be asked where sovereignty lies, for example, in the United States. The national government is not the sovereign lawmaker, for certain powers are reserved to the states and these may not be taken away. Within the national government, the President and the two chambers of the legislature must all participate in enacting laws. It cannot be said that any one of the three branches is "supreme." Moreover, the Supreme Court may overrule statutes and nullify executive orders. But it does not have the last word because the composition of and the rules governing the court's jurisdiction are subject to legislative revision. All these relationships can be altered if the states amend the Constitution, and some observers have found "sovereignty" in the legislatures or conventions that have this power. But it has only been exercised twenty-two times and not on issues of the most crucial character. One might then conclude that the people of America are the sovereign because they elect or control the makers of public policy. However, this begs

[9] *Ibid.*, p. 173.

the question of which people we are talking about and at which times. For the people only participate in the lawmaking process in specified ways and at certain junctures. Perhaps the Constitution itself is the sovereign; however, a little reflection shows that it is a piece of parchment always standing in need of interpretation.

The real answer is that sovereignty is not something that can be identified or discovered. It is, on the contrary, a *process*. In other words, it is the interaction of specified individuals and institutions according to specified rules of procedure. Laws are only enacted, cases are only decided, and constitutions are only amended if certain paths of action are followed by people in a certain accredited position. The process of sovereignty, therefore, is more concerned with *how* laws are passed than with *what* they say. This is why many theorists believe that a constitution must be the foundation of any government. For such a document lays down the basic rules by which laws are made and attempts to ensure that the whims and caprices of politicians are checked by orderly procedures.

WHO HAS THE POWER? "In all republics, however organized," one theorist writes, "there are never more than forty or fifty citizens who attain a position that entitles them to command."[10] This view suggests that while lawyers may muse over questions of legality and sovereignty, the key issue is who has the real power in politics. Even in the best of democracies, where the people believe that they govern themselves, it can still be suggested that power gravitates (or ascends) to a small elite. Indeed, even in a representative system where lawmakers are popularly elected it can be shown that a ruling coterie emerges. Constitutions, therefore, are less important than the men who are able to shape them in ways of their own choosing. Legislatures may enact laws according to specified procedures, but the real issue is which individuals and groups secure laws that promote their own interests.

The elite theory is based on several premises, all worth considering. The first is that the mass of the people is usually apathetic about politics. They do not want to govern themselves and would not know how to do so even if they wanted to. All that the people need, this view proceeds, is material security and a sense of self-respect. If the economic

[10] Niccolo Machiavelli, *Discourse on the First Ten Books of Titus Livius,* in *The Prince and the Discourses*, Modern Library, Random House, Inc., New York, 1940, p. 163.

well-being of a population can be achieved, then its ego can be boosted by flattery and the manipulation of patriotic and kindred symbols. Indeed, most citizens *want* to be followers and they are grateful when authoritative leaders appear on the scene. Coincidental with all of these tendencies is the fact that as political life becomes organized certain "laws" come into play. That is, popular movements turn into organized parties and these in turn become rigid bureaucracies. The same evolution occurs in government itself and with other social institutions. The making of decisions develops into a specialized process, and only those with expert information can participate in a serious way. Thus leaders become a select group, separated from the average citizens and possessed of disproportionate power. Who are these leaders? As was pointed out in an earlier chapter, they may have one of several aptitudes. One such leader will have a talent for projecting his personality and amassing a following around him as an individual. Another may be an able administrator, with the ability to execute far-reaching policies by manipulating a complex organization. But the point is that no matter what the country or the period in history, this theory asserts that effective power will always be in a few hands. This means that democracy, defined as popular self-government, is a myth. However, it does not mean that all governments are tyrannies. For an oligarchic system need not oppress the mass of citizens, and the best of them will make an explicit point not to do so.

Governments must exercise power and most will agree that such power should be wielded by rational men. The real argument comes over the question whether men of reason form only a small minority or if there is a sufficiency of reason in the community at large to allow for attempts at self-government. This issues lies at the heart of the controversy over democracy, and that theory should be turned to next.

Review Questions

1. Is government the only institution that can deprive an individual of his freedom?

2. How can someone be "forced to be free"?

3. Can a person think he is free and yet not be?

4. How can men be considered equal despite obvious differences in attributes and achievements?

5. What is the difference between a right and a privilege?

6. Is there one person, or group of persons, in a society who may be said to be sovereign?

IDEOLOGIES AND INTERESTS

Chapter 4

Properly understood, political theory bears a close connection to the important issues of political life. It is often tempting for students of politics to preoccupy themselves with the trivial, if only because the more minute a subject is the easier it is to handle. By the same token, there is a tendency to delve into conditions and conflicts of the political past, for those controversies have been settled and may be described without undue difficulty. In addition, there are commentators who concentrate on questions of current or topical concern, selecting these problems because they happen to arouse popular and often undiscriminating interest. These pitfalls must be avoided. If political theory is to serve a serious purpose then it must discuss serious issues. That is, it must focus on questions that recur in political life and which transcend the particular experience of particular societies and epochs.

This is more easily said than done. For the significant problems of politics cannot always be analyzed or evaluated in a dispassionate way. A theorist, in theory at least, serves only a single master: truth. His self-imposed mission is to describe how and explain why politics operates as it does. He is also obliged to outline how politics ought to be conducted if the general welfare is to be maintained and promoted. The dilemma for would-be theorists is that their propositions tend to be diluted by *ideology*.

The more important a political issue becomes, the more likely it will be that ideology will intrude itself into theory. This is inevitable. There can be no such thing as "pure" theory or "pure" ideology, although some pamphleteers come pretty close to approximating the latter. What must be said, in consequence, is that anyone who reads the literature of politics must be on constant guard. He must be able to detect ideological intrusions and to ask how and why they managed to creep in. This warning is especially important in the case of the theories that are to follow. For it is all but impossible to discuss democracy, welfare, and revolution in a dispassionate tone. Emotions and interests, distortions and rationalizations are constantly at play in this arena. Nor is this to be deplored or condemned out of hand. The intervention of these altogether human qualities gives life to the debate and reminds us once again that serious men think these questions important. They are.

THE DEBATE OVER DEMOCRACY

MOB RULE "When the poor win, the result is democracy," one theorist writes. "They will kill some of the opposite party, banish others, and grant the rest an equal share in civil rights and government."[1] This theory, a popular one throughout history, defines democracy as mob rule. Every society has more poor people than rich people, more who are uneducated than who are educated. If political power is distributed equally throughout the population, then sheer quantity of numbers will win out over quality. The populace, led by leaders much like themselves but talented in the arts of demagogy, will overwhelm the cul-

[1] Plato, *The Republic* (translated by Francis M. Cornford), Oxford University Press, Fair Lawn, N. J., 1945, p. 282.

tured, the well-to-do, and the well-born minorities that previously had high status in the community. The masses, furthermore, are unable or unwilling to appreciate the values that such minorities have promoted or the functions they performed on behalf of all of society. Hence, there results not simply majority rule, but a "tyranny of the majority."

Democracy in this form does not have to be accompanied by violence. The redistribution of power can be a gradual process, each decade giving more of a say to the average citizen and his neighbors. In the same way the expropriation of property, the dilution of privilege, and the downgrading of culture may take place by stages rather than at one seizure. The gradual growth of equalitarian democracy is a subtle development and it is difficult to draw a line in arguing that the people have too much power. Yet once the majority secures new rights it is virtually impossible to withdraw them.

DOES THE MOB RULE? At the same time it is argued that popular democracy usually has a short life and it seldom allows majority rule for an extended period. "The people always put forward a single champion of their interests, whom they nurse to greatness," the same theorist writes. "Here, plainly enough, is the root from which despotism invariably springs."[2] A mob, in actual fact, is poorly equipped for conducting the business of government. Whether its members are roaming the streets, gathered in the marketplace, or sitting in their homes they cannot make policy or carry out programs. The experience has been that a single man or a small group of men are elevated to positions of leadership, and from this eminence they presumably exercise power in the name of the people. Is such a popular leader a "despot"? He looks that way to those citizens who have suffered from the advent of democracy. But to the populace he may be a hero, a savior, even a saint whose likeness looks down from every wall. However, as he or his successors consolidate the fruits of popular rule, he may be ruthless to those who were once in the vanguard of democracy but who now oppose certain methods or personalities. But as long as the leaders have the support of the masses they usually have a free hand in selecting their lieutenants and administering the governmental apparatus.

The conclusion must be that democracy and despotism are not incompatible. An oligarchic ruler may be raised to power by the majority and kept there by their loyalty and enthusiasm. What he must

[2] *Ibid.*, p. 291.

remember is that real power lies in the people, that their sensibilities must be flattered and their material condition improved. This kind of democracy, then, *is* in the final analysis a form of self-government. Leaders "represent" their followings after a fashion and the masses feel that their interests are being attended to. Such a democracy has little room for individual dissenters or opposition parties. Nor can it contain deliberative legislatures or an independent judiciary. What must be said is that if it has a popular base, the people who make up this constituency take a fairly rudimentary view of politics and a rather unsophisticated view of human freedom. But as most people in the world are of this sort it ought not to be surprising that popular democracy, coupled with authoritarian leadership, is a popular form of government.

THE RATIONAL MAJORITY   "There is this to be said for the Many," another theorist writes. "Each of them by himself may not be of a good quality; but when they all come together it is possible that they may surpass—collectively and as a body, although not individually— the quality of the best few."[3] The previous juxtaposition had been between the Few and the Many, between the minority and the majority. On the one hand there were the well-to-do, the well-born, and the cultured. On the other there were the poor, the humbly born, and the philistine. The majority was regarded as the natural enemy of the various minorities alongside them in society. Moreover, the majority was considered incompetent to govern, being unable to appreciate the finer things of life or to take a long-range view on questions of public policy. The new approach suggests that the Many, when considered as a collectivity, possesses a wisdom of its own that may be superior to that of any minority. For one thing, it has been pointed out that there may be several minority groups in the community, each of which styles itself as being of superior quality. Quite frequently the minority of the rich will clash in a serious way with the minority of the intellectuals on what constitute rational courses of action. By allowing the majority to govern, the problem of deciding which of various minorities is "really" superior is avoided.

How can one find wisdom or rationality in the majority? For this group lacks education, often inclines to excess, and has been known to select as its leaders the most irresponsible of demagogues. The an-

[3] Aristotle, *Politics* (translated by Ernest Baker), Oxford University Press, Fair Lawn, N. J., 1946, p. 123.

swer is to be found, first of all, by returning to a theory of human nature. It is acknowledged that the majority has, on occasion, acted as a tyrant when it secures power. But this is only because it was itself long a victim of exploitation, and the exploiter–exploited relationship is the one it has learned to understand. The members of the majority have, in other words, been corrupted; it is understandable that in such circumstances they choose the leaders that they do. Once the experience of exploitation has been removed, this theory proceeds, the goodness and rationality inherent in the common man has a chance to develop. These qualities rise to their heights, furthermore, when men deliberate collectively. For in the course of discussion they exchange facts and ideas and also come to appreciate the interests and opinions of others. In this way the majority emerges with a sense of what its own needs are and, hopefully, what is best for society as a whole.

ARISTOCRATIC LEADERS AND DEMOCRATIC FOLLOWERS? "No government," one theorist writes, " . . . ever did or could rise above mediocrity, except in so far as the sovereign Many have let themselves be guided (which in their best times they have always done) by the counsels and influence of a more highly gifted and instructed One or Few."[4] Here the thought is expressed that the majority has frequently shown itself willing to pick as leaders the best minds and talents in society. And they have done this even though those leaders come from a different class or ethnic group than themselves. In these cases the common man is displaying a commendable deference to his betters. He acknowledges his own limitations, and he willingly places men of superior abilities in positions of power. Thus, if one speaks of the good sense of the majority, part of what is meant is that the ordinary citizens have the wisdom to know quality when they see it and to elevate it to places of leadership.

This conception of democracy, therefore, had best be called "representative democracy" in contradistinction to the popular democracy that was discussed before. In a representative democracy the people have the right to vote, and on the whole they allow the men they place in office to make policy and run the government. That is, citizens are content to elect their rulers and to pass judgment on them at subsequent elections. But between elections the majority permits its representatives to do what they think best. The majority, in this system,

[4] John Stuart Mill, *On Liberty*, in *Utilitarianism, Liberty, and Representative Government*, J. M. Dent & Sons, Ltd., Publishers, London, 1910, p. 124.

must *not* have intense opinions on every political issue, and it must refrain from rising as a mass movement in an effort to exert pressure on elected officeholders. A degree of such pressure is permissible, to remind representatives of their constituents' sentiments, but it must not get out of hand. The reason for this is that lawmakers and administrators have to be able to give reasoned consideration to policies and programs, and they cannot be stampeded by the public clamor of the moment. Indeed, if superior men are selected for office then they should be allowed to exercise their knowledge and intelligence in an atmosphere of calm and objectivity. Moreover, within legislative assemblies the representatives of various classes and regions will be able, in a peaceable way, to compromise and perhaps reconcile the conflicting interests that are always present in politics.

MAJORITY RULE VERSUS MINORITY RIGHTS   "For a people that governs and is well regulated by laws will be stable, prudent and grateful, as much so, and even more, according to my opinion, than a prince," one theorist writes.[5] While it is well to have faith in the stability, prudence, and gratitude of the majority it is also important to ensure that majority power is regulated by certain basic laws. The notion that a representative democracy is a republican form of government also implies that the entire political system is overarched by a constitution that protects individual liberty and minority rights. The power of the majority, therefore, is not unlimited. There are certain things that neither the majority nor its elected representatives are allowed to do. These restrictions are intended to protect citizens from oppression at the hands of their neighbors. Nevertheless, such constitutional guarantees will only survive if the members of the majority are reasonably tolerant of dissenters and properly deferential to the institutions that seek to uphold the rights of individuals. When such tolerance and deference is not forthcoming, the whole theory of limited majority rule is in jeopardy.

Which rights of individuals and minorities can legitimately claim constitutional protection? This is one of the great controversies of democratic theory. The well-to-do may assert that they have a right to keep all the money they have earned or inherited. Political dissenters may claim that they have a right to clamor for radical changes in the social

[5] Niccolo Machiavelli, *Discourses on the First Ten Books of Titus Livius,* in *The Prince and the Discourses,* Modern Library, Random House, Inc., 1940, p. 262.

and governmental system. Intellectuals may insist that the accoutrements of high culture deserve disproportionately greater support and encouragement. All these minority assertions tend to fly in the face of majority sentiment, and it is difficult to know which of the claims deserve to be respected. One of the reasons why courts of justice are supposed to be independent of political pressures is that they can decide who has what rights without having to worry about the majority opinion of the moment. But even judges must keep one ear cocked to public feeling, for they cannot grant or withhold rights in ways that clash too resoundingly with popular conceptions of justice. This is, in sum, a recurring problem of democracy. It is never "solved," but the process of reconciling majority rule and minority rights is a series of adjustments on the part of all parties concerned.

PROMOTING THE GENERAL WELFARE

No one is "against" welfare. It is impossible to discover a reputable theorist who believes that poverty is to be praised or misery eulogized. The real question concerns the ways and means of promoting the general welfare. If the poor and underprivileged are looked on as a "problem," the arguments are over which of various solutions best coincides with the values of justice and progress. And while the substantive issue may be economic in character, it is clear that political policies play a key role. For the economy and the system of government stand in integral relations to one another, and the contours of one will inevitably be shaped by the outlines of the other.

PROPERTY, PERSONALITY, AND PROGRESS "The great and chief end of men's uniting into commonwealths, and putting themselves under government, is the preservation of their property," one theorist writes.[6] According to this view the freedom to own property is a "natural" right belonging to all citizens and it is the obligation of government to guarantee that right. This theory of property is very much bound up with the idea that each individual ought to develop his own personality. However, if he is to express himself as a free man he must have some minimum of economic security. The property owner can, by building up possessions that are uniquely his own, create not only a source of livelihood but also a defensive bulwark against the rest of society. That

[6] John Locke, *Second Treatise of Civil Government*, in E. A. Burtt (ed.), *The English Philosophers from Bacon to Mill*, Modern Library, Random House, Inc., New York, 1939, par. 124.

is, the man of property has in effect a "fenced-off" area where he can do what he wants as he pleases. In addition, it is through his private property that an individual can express his personality. He can build a business or farm his land in ways of his own devising, thus imposing his character on an enterprise in a unique manner. Related to this is the fact that through property a person can secure a sense of "identity." In an organic society this identity comes to an individual through his family inheritance and by his fulfilling a settled role in the community. In an atomistic society, however, identity is more difficult to establish because attachments are transitory and roles in a constant state of flux. But through the ownership of property an individual can shape an identity for himself by merging his personality with his business or land, thus creating a focus by which others know him and by which, indeed, he comes to know himself. Owning property, then, is not simply an economic right. It also brings in its train psychological benefits of profound importance.

For this reason government must protect the right of citizens to acquire and own property. The state should remain aloof from the economic realm, permitting individuals to buy and sell and build their fortunes. Only in a marketplace unhampered by government regulation can each person exercise his talents and express his personality. Furthermore, by refraining from intervening the government is actually promoting economic progress. Through free competition, prices are kept low and the quality of service grows better. Because innovation is a matter of individual decisions, new products develop and more jobs are created. Entrepreneurs take risks and there are penalties for the losers as well as rewards for the winners. However, the overall result is a rising standard of living for everyone and an increase in the wealth of nations. Thus, while there may be poor as well as rich, the material level of the poor is constantly rising to new heights. In addition, new individuals can begin new enterprises, thus using their talents to better their condition. Such an economy provides incentives for progress and, by its workings, serves the welfare of all.

AN ECONOMIC ROLE FOR GOVERNMENT   "The business of government is to promote the happiness of society," another theorist writes. And this includes "the power which takes for its object the introduction of positive good."[7] Why is it suggested that the government must take

---

[7] Jeremy Bentham, *The Principles of Morals and Legislation*, in Wilfrid Harrison (ed.), *A Fragment on Government and the Principles of Morals and Legislation*, Basil Blackwell & Mott, Ltd., Oxford, 1948, pp. 189, 323.

a "positive" role in the economy? The reply to this question is that the workings of the free market may or may not provide a rising standard of living for everyone, poor as well as rich. But what does emerge is that in most societies the benefits of property ownership accrue only to a minority. Not everyone has sufficient talent or good fortune to become a successful entrepreneur. And those whose rewards are comparatively meager are not usually happy about the workings of the competitive system. Moreover, those who have done less well often constitute the majority and they may use political means to redress the unequal balance in the economy. Nor will it do to point out that the society itself is progressing, that the standard of living has been rising. For most people set their expectations by observing the condition of life of those better off than themselves and they are not mollified by statistical tables telling them they "never had it so good" before. In addition to this it is frequently argued that the free market does not always provide jobs for everyone who wants to work, and even if it does it does not always supply essential services. The sum of this analysis is that government must play a positive role in the economy, with the occasional afterthought that whether or not it should it is probably going to do so anyway.

The economic functions can be varied. They may involve the redistribution of wealth, by taxing the well-to-do and with this money providing free or low-cost services to the poor. Other roles may entail regulating the market by telling businessmen what they must do or cannot do, the intention being to create a more rational system of production and distribution. Here the assumption is that an "invisible hand" does *not* automatically produce prosperity, that the visible hand of government must act as a referee and often as a rule-maker. On occasion too, agencies of government will enter the marketplace, manufacturing goods and supplying services that private citizens are unable or unwilling to provide. In all these instances the theory is that the government is an agency of service rather than a wielder of oppressive power. The idea is that while a few businessmen and others may be harmed by redistributive or regulatory measures, this is amply compensated for by the many citizens who gain greater security in the process. And only if they have such security can they begin to experience the good life themselves and give a good start to their children.

PROPERTY AND THE PROPERTYLESS The right to property, while in theory open to all, in practice is meaningful only to a portion of the population. The role that government is to play in the economic realm, whether it is to be active or passive, in the final analysis depends on the attitude of the citizens who are *not* property owners in a serious sense. If they are relatively satisfied with their share of the rewards offered by the marketplace, then they will not use their votes or their power to encourage government intervention. However, if they are not satisfied, then they will seek to employ governmental authority as a positive force. Citizens devise their own conceptions of economic progress and social justice, and it is not an easy matter to persuade them that these notions may perhaps be short-sighted or misguided. Whether the rights of property ownership will be safeguarded depends, in the final analysis, on how many citizens feel that their welfare is being promoted by the unregulated workings of the marketplace. If a majority feels that they are suffering injustice then the chances are good that government intervention will ultimately be forthcoming. One of the consequences of democracy is that people seek to solve their economic problems by political means. And the existence of economic problems, it must never be forgotten, is one of the reasons why democracy itself has emerged as an ideology and as a system of government.

OBEDIENCE, OPPRESSION, AND REVOLUTION

OBEDIENCE TO AUTHORITY "It would indeed be dangerous, both for the community and for its rulers, if individuals were, upon private initiative, to attempt the death of those who govern, albeit tyrannically," one theorist writes. "The consequence of such presumption is more likely to be the loss of a good king to the community than any benefit from the suppression of tyranny."[8] The argument against disobedience —whether it involves merely ignoring a traffic signal or embarking upon a course of violent revolution—is a powerful one. One of the most important characteristics of government, whether it is benevolent or tyrannical, is that it is a means of preserving order. All men want society to be an orderly place. They want to live under a system of rules and they want life to be reasonably predictable. Citizens like to know that the mail will be delivered on time, that police will protect them from criminals, that their currency will buy tomorrow pretty much what it bought today. Any individual, or group of individuals, who

[8] St. Thomas Aquinas, *On Princely Government,* in A. P. D'Entreves (ed.), *Aquinas, Selected Political Writings* (translated by J. G. Dawson), Basil Blackwell & Mott, Ltd., Oxford, 1954, p. 31.

undertakes to disobey the law or to overthrow the government is, whether he realizes it or not, threatening an edifice upon which civilized life is built. A legal and political structure takes years, even generations and centuries, to create. The obligation to obey authority is often annoying and sometimes it requires putting up with no small degree of injustice. However, disobedience can bring consequences that are harmful not only to society but also to the individuals who first thought that the overthrow of tyranny would bring them freedom and justice.

For if disobedience is condoned, then bad men may break good laws no less than may good men break bad ones. If revolution is sanctioned, then good rulers may be toppled no less than tyrants. If citizens are granted a "right of revolution" then it should not be surprising that all who foment rebellion will claim that they are acting under this right. Moreover, disobedience weakens the whole fabric of law, and revolution destroys not only tyranny but also the institutions of government that make for stability and order. The aftermath of revolution is usually marked by the rise of a new autocracy that proceeds to deprive whole groups and classes of their liberty. In sum, revolutions seldom if ever fulfill their promises. Old tyrants are replaced by new and the freedom won by some is paid for by the injustice visited on others.

Only a few societies in history and even in the world today are so organized that political change can take place without violence. Only a handful of nations have regular elections at which, under a meaningful party system, citizens may replace their rules in an orderly manner. By the same token it is only in these states that the man in the street can work to have bad laws repealed and ones more to his liking enacted. Hence, rather than engage in civil disobedience he will put up with laws he finds distasteful, in the hope that by banding with others of similar persuasion he can eventually persuade the legislators to amend the statutes. In most parts of the world, however, there are not such channels for change. This means that the question of whether or not to obey is ever-present. It also means that the threat of revolution can never be ignored. For despite the cogency of the argument for obedience, the forces of discontent are both extensive and persuasive. Indeed, the causes of revolution comprise one of the key questions in political theory.

WHY MEN REVOLT "At a certain stage of their development, the material productive forces of society come into conflict with the existing relations of production . . ." another theorist writes. "Then begins an epoch of social revolution."[9] This, the most famous of all revolutionary theories, explains social and political upheaval by analyzing the economic and technological elements in human relationships. According to Marxist theory, there are periods in history when the stage of technological development ("the material productive forces") are in harmony with the way in which the economy ("the existing relations of production") is organized. That is, the feudal economic system is well-suited to a primitive agricultural technology. Or a capitalist economic system harmonizes with small-scale manufacturing and a technology based on steam power. At such intervals in history the workers see no injustice in an economy where only a few own property, because that particular kind of economy seems to go best with the technological instruments at hand. Trouble arises, this theory goes on to say, when the workers begin to perceive an inherent conflict between the "forces" of production and the "relations" of production. What happens is that, as technology advances, the workers become more sophisticated and they begin to sense a certain irrationality in the system. If they work in a capitalist economy, for example, they may begin to ask why they labor for a pittance whereas others who do not work reap the profits. Indeed, they may begin to conclude that whereas the factory is a rational agency of production, the way in which the economy is organized is lacking in logic. In order to bring things into harmony once more, the workers organize a revolutionary movement. The purpose of the revolution is to displace those in power and to replace them with a system that is compatible with the emerging technology. It is wrong to call Marxist theory an "economic determinism." If anything, it is a "technological determinism." It is not capitalism as an economic system that makes men revolutionaries. Rather it is the machines, the factories, and the processes of production that shape their minds and foster their discontents.

This theory, then, is an attempt to explain why citizens become dissatisfied with prevailing social and political arrangements. It is a theory of history and also a psychological theory, and no one will deny that it has been singularly influential over the past 100 years. The Marxist analysis assumes that the property-owning minority (the bourgeoisie) exploits the propertyless majority (the proletariat). However, it may

[9] Karl Marx, Preface to *A Contribution to the Critique of Political Economy*, in *Marx and Engels: Selected Works*, Foreign Languages Publishing House, Moscow, 1951, 1958, vol. I, p. 363.

take a long time before the majority even realizes it is being exploited; indeed they will only come to this realization once they develop a sense of "class consciousness." What makes them class conscious is the impact of their work on their lives; constant exposure to the forces of technology defines their role in society.

Most commentators acknowledge that the Marxist explanation of revolution is not the whole one. For one thing, the important revolutions of our time have taken place in nonindustrial societies. In these instances the workers were not exposed to a mass production technology and had no chance to juxtapose the "rationality" of the machine with the "irrationality" of capitalist ownership. If a feeling of exploitation has emerged in the minds of the majority it stems from other bases. One of these is nationalism, the growing desire on the part of emerging societies to throw off their foreign overlords and to govern themselves. The forces of nationalism and anticolonialism are political rather than economic. Although exploitation remains a major theme, the exploiters are alien rulers rather than domestic capitalists.

THE SEARCH FOR STABILITY   "Not only are the men of democracies not naturally desirous of revolutions, but they are afraid of them," another theorist writes. "All revolutions more or less threaten the tenure of property; but most of those who live in democratic countries are possessed of property."[10] Most democratic societies are also industrialized, and these nations have experienced the expansion of the middle class as a social group. Indeed, in some of these countries the working class is actually becoming a minority and those who are affected by poverty form a very small section of the community. The way to achieve stability, to avoid revolution, is to give as many citizens as possible a vested interest in preserving the *status quo.* By extending property ownership and prosperity to the majority discontents are erased and the forces of protest are deprived of a coherent program.

But this, too, is an economic explanation of political stability. Whether they own property or not, individuals still want to feel that they are governing themselves. They want to participate in the processes whereby policy is made and power is exercised. Consequently, a democracy must have not only a fair degree of economic equality but also political equality. Citizens should be able to take part in selecting

[10] Alexis de Tocqueville, *Democracy in America* (translated by Henry Reeve), Phillips Bradley (ed.), Vintage Books, Random House, Inc., New York, vol. II, p. 267.

the men who will rule them and they should be able to influence the laws under which they live. Presumably if men can cast ballots they will not have to use bullets to remove their rulers from office. Or, to shift the metaphor, if decisions are made by counting heads then they will not have to be enforced by breaking heads. However, a stable society and democratic government are not secured simply because political theorists say they are the best way of ordering human relationships. The roads to stability and democracy are difficult paths to pursue. It is therefore of some use to turn from the classical texts of political theory and to see how at least one nation embarked upon this venture.

Review Questions

1. If democracy is viewed as the tyranny of the majority, who are the tyrants and who are the tyrannized?

2. What is the difference between popular democracy and representative democracy?

3. Why is the right of private property thought to be important?

4. When does the government intervene in the economy?

5. Have citizens any obligation to obey their government?

6. What causes revolutions?

HUMAN NATURE AND POLITICAL AUTHORITY

Chapter 5

Many commentators lament the fact that there are no American political theorists comparable to those produced by the European tradition. Great Britain can claim Locke, Burke, Bentham, Hobbes, and Mill. France has given us Rousseau and de Tocqueville. Germany, to its credit or not, may point to Hegel and Marx. And Italy has Machiavelli.

Somehow or for some reason the theoretical impulse has failed to flower in American soil. There are explanations for this state of affairs. It may be said that we are a young nation, and that in the fullness of time there will develop creative minds and audiences receptive to mature ideas. It can be suggested that Americans have been preoccupied in building a continent, and the practical aspects of life are necessarily emphasized. Nor can it be denied that during the past century both America and the world have been in an unsettled condition, and a theory written today may well be obsolete by tomorrow.

PHILOSOPHY PLUS PROPAGANDA Nevertheless, Americans have no reason to be apologetic. *The Federalist*, written at the birth of the Republic in 1787 and 1788, may be regarded as a major contribution to political theory. There is, to be sure, some understandable hesitation about placing it on a shelf alongside the august books of the European tradition. For one thing, *The Federalist* originated not as a book but as a series of newspaper articles. And these articles had not a single author but rather three authors, each of whom put forward his own ideas in his separate contributions to the series. Thus, *The Federalist* may be criticized for being aimed at a large and popular audience, for being put together hurriedly to meet newspaper deadlines, for embracing varied and even opposing viewpoints due to multiple authorship. Yet the overriding fact is that in spite of these handicaps the articles—not properly regarded as a book—contain ideas of major and lasting significance for politics. Indeed, the pressures operating on the authors worked to bring out the best in them, and that in itself is a lesson of no small importance.

The Constitutional Convention met in the summer of 1787, and it succeeded in drawing up a document that would transform 13 loosely confederated states into a single federal republic. Upon the adjournment of that gathering the delegates dispersed, and not a few of them turned their attention to the practical business of getting the document ratified. One of the key states, then as now, was New York. To convince the voters of New York that they should support the proposed constitution a major campaign of popular persuasion was necessary. In consequence, John Jay, Alexander Hamilton, and James Madison set pen to paper and wrote 85 articles for publication in various New York newspapers. These frankly propagandistic columns had as their purpose winning votes for the new constitution. All the articles were brief and all were anonymous. Each one was signed "Publius," but we are now able to assign authorship to the individual papers. We know that Hamilton was responsible for 51 of them, that Madison wrote 26, that Jay wrote 5, and that 3 were collaborative efforts by the two principal authors.

Reading these articles raises some fascinating questions about the art of political persuasion. As has been noted, these were newspaper columns and were clearly aimed at a large and quite ordinary reading public. After all, ratification of the Constitution in New York State would be in the hands of an electorate of significant proportions. Though not all adult males were able to vote, the franchise still embraced many citizens of humble background and limited education. Yet the articles contain all manner of academic and historical allusions. There are references to writers like Plato, Montesquieu, Grotius, and Hume; there are discussions of ancient Greece, Renaissance Italy, and Reformation England. The modern reader may well wonder about the presumed sophistication of the average newspaper buyer in 1788, and he cannot help but compare the elevated level of the *Federalist* arguments with the superficial mode of discussion that prevails today. There are, as will be seen, extended analyses of major questions of political theory such as human nature, social structure, and governmental authority. How much of this was comprehensible to the citizen newspaper reader of New York? We do not really know. But what can be said is that the *Federalist* authors also devoted ample space to the practical and emotional considerations that clearly concerned the voters. If they waxed philosophical, they also went far to allay the fears that a unitary national government would destroy the powers of the states. If they drew their analogies from history, they also proceeded to demonstrate that the new constitution would bring order and prosperity to an emerging nation.

In contrast to the ideas of the European tradition that have been discussed, *The Federalist* has a direct link with specific political institutions and social conditions. That is, the authors were content to deal with problems that were discretely American. They did not prescribe conduct or institutions for all men everywhere. The Constitution was an American instrument, with institutions designed to solve American problems in an American context. The upshot is that the theories in *The Federalist* were never far removed from practical matters of government and politics. A generalization about human nature, for example, was to be used to justify a bicameral legislature. A reflection on political authority was to be offered as a rationalization for a unitary executive. *The Federalist*, therefore, served as a bridge between theory and practice. And it was because its authors were men who combined scholarly learning and practical experience that such a transition could be effected.

A SPLIT PERSONALITY? John Jay's five papers are of little importance and will not be treated here. The bulk of *The Federalist* was written by Alexander Hamilton and James Madison. Can it be said that two authors, writing collaboratively, are able to produce a single theory? This was the case with Marx and Engels, and yet it was clearly Marx who provided the inspiration. While Engels was a person of great talent, he accepted his master's theoretical framework in all important particulars. Hamilton and Madison were men with minds of their own, and they did not agree on all subjects. While they shared a view of human nature and the social structure, they parted company when it came to saying what ought to be the respective roles of the state and the individual in the good society. Hamilton's main theme was that the national government be strong and authoritative; he cared little for the rights of the states and he was surprisingly unconcerned about the liberties of individuals. In his theoretical scheme national power was at the center of things. With Madison the emphasis was much more on the representation of local sentiment and the protection of citizens' rights. For him individual freedom was of central importance. On this basis it has been argued that *The Federalist* is actually a "split personality," that there are two theories on its pages rather than one.

The real answer is more complicated. Hamilton knew his own mind and his own theory is both forceful and internally consistent. Madison, on the other hand, tended to waver between agreement with Hamilton's emphasis on national power and his own preoccupation with individual freedom. If there is a "split personality" it is to be found in Madison himself, not in *The Federalist* as a whole. This interpretation will become clear as the actual arguments of the book are set forth.

Constitutions are written for the real political world. They are not drawn up to "prove" a political theory or to impose some philosophical framework upon the citizens of a nation. The framers who met in Philadelphia were practical statesmen. If they were men of learning, and they were, they put their classical educations to one side in their attempts to create a workable constitution for the new United States. At the same time this constitution had to operate in a human and social context. Such a context is not created *by* a theory but rather develops as a product of culture and history. Nevertheless, men and societies can only be *understood* if they are viewed in the light of theory. This the *Federalist* authors well knew, and they made clear their underlying assumptions as they propounded the arguments for the Constitution.

REALISM AND RATIONALITY

THE ATTACK ON UTOPIA Both Madison and Hamilton stressed the limited and imperfect character of human nature. There are repeated references to "ambition," "avarice," "passion," "vindictiveness," "rapacity," "rage," "resentment," "jealousy," "contention," and "irrationality" on the pages of *The Federalist*. Hamilton had the greater tendency to underscore these traits. "A man must be far gone in Utopian speculations," he wrote in No. 6, ". . . to forget that men are ambitious, vindictive, and rapacious." Even those who seem, at first glance, to adhere to the path of reason can be attacked on the grounds of harboring irrational motives. "Ambition, avarice, personal animosity, party opposition, and many other motives not more laudable than these," Hamilton wrote in No. 1, "are apt to operate as well upon those who support as those who oppose the right side of a question." From the outset the *Federalist* authors sought to establish that the proposed constitution would deal with men as they are and as they have been throughout human history. "If men were angels, no government would be necessary," Madison said in No. 51. But Americans are not angels, and while the Constitution was an instrument that would alter the structure of government, it could do nothing to change the fundamental instincts of individuals. Indeed, Hamilton was fearful that a Utopian frame of mind would work great harm on any effort to create a viable government. "Is it not time," he asked in No. 6, "to awake from the deceitful dream of a golden age and to adopt as a practical maxim for the direction of our political conduct that we, as well as other inhabitants of the globe, are yet remote from the happy empire of perfect wisdom and perfect virtue?"

To speak of the imperfect wisdom and virtue of men is to imply that there will always exist people who are ignorant and people who are perverse. At no time will all men have complete knowledge nor will there ever be universal agreement on the means and ends of public policy. The minds and behavior of citizens are continually distorted and corrupted by self-interest, and this in the face of all attempts to promote the general welfare. "As long as the reason of man continues fallible, and he is at liberty to exercise it, different opinions will be formed," Madison said in No. 10. And out of the differences of opinions will rise conflicts and tensions that must be curbed because they cannot be eradicated. The outlook of Hamilton and Madison then, was one that accepts the doctrine of original sin; there is, they assumed, a perverse streak in mankind that prevents all efforts to create a harmonious society. "Has it not invariably been found," Hamilton again asked in No. 6, "that momentary passions, and immediate interests, have a more active and impervious control over human conduct than general or remote considerations of policy, utility, or justice?" To this question both the *Federalist* authors answered an unreserved "Yes."

WHEN MEN FOREGATHER   Original sin is more than a theory of human nature. It is also a theory of group behavior. There may be some reason for believing that men, if they are taken singly as individuals, are potentially rational creatures and are capable of altruistic behavior. For example, the writers of *The Federalist* would not have addressed their arguments to the newspaper readers of New York had they not believed in some measure that these citizens might be persuaded by the force of logic and an impressive array of facts. However, the act of reading is highly personal; it is really a private conversation between author and reader. The implication is that human reason is most evident when the individual is isolated from his fellow citizens. But when men enter groups they become part of an atmosphere that tends to destroy whatever rational qualities its members might have possessed as individuals. This theory is especially relevant in politics, because legislative assemblies are common institutions of government. "Are not popular assemblies frequently subject to the impulses of rage, resentment, jealousy, avarice, and of other irregular and violent propensities?" Hamilton asked in No. 6. This was a rhetorical question, but if he needed an answer it was supplied by Madison in No. 38:

> The history of almost all the great councils and consultations held among mankind for reconciling their discordant opinions, assuaging their mutual jealousies and adjusting their respective interests, is a history of factions, contentions, and disappointments, and may be classed among the most dark and degraded pictures which display the infirmities and depravities of the human character.

While the legislative branch of government will have the authority to make a nation's laws, it must itself be subject to controls so that the assembled passions of its members are held in check. The difference between a legislature and a street-corner mob is one of degree. Both display the irrationalities that arise when men meet and act collectively.

LIMITING POWER

Human perversity and the clash of interests pervade the social scene. Men are creatures who cannot be trusted, and groups stand in need of external controls. It follows that the function of government is to provide a groundwork of order. For without order there can be no serious talk of liberty or equality or justice. The proposed constitution, a 7,000-word document laying down the form the new government was to take, was itself testimony that political behavior could not be left to chance. If the Constitution had a purpose it was to specify who was to have power and on what occasions those exercises of power might be deemed legitimate. If such a document did not exist as the supreme law of the land, then the country would be left with only the hope that wise rulers might appear on the scene and that they would reconcile human differences and govern society rationally. The likelihood of the emergence of philosopher-kings, though noble as a theory, could not form a practical basis for the strife-torn America that confronted the *Federalist* authors. "It is vain to say that enlightened statesmen will be able to adjust these clashing interests and render them all subservient to the public good," Madison said in No. 10. "Enlightened statesmen will not always be at the helm." What was needed was a concrete constitutional document, a legal instrument which would be the supreme law of the land, that would provide in a specific way what was to be the allocation of power.

The theory of original sin of Hamilton and Madison extended not simply over the general citizenry and the members of legislative assemblies, but to all who might hold governmental office. Their axiom, quite frankly put, was that no one was to be trusted. But men are not without ways and means of dealing with this situation. The framers of the proposed constitution began by providing for the dispersion of power into three branches of government. Hamilton described this principle in No. 9:

> The science of politics, however, like most other sciences, has received great improvement. The efficacy of various principles is now well understood, which were either not known at all, or imperfectly known to the ancients. The regular distribution of

> power into distinct departments . . . are means, and
> powerful means, by which the excellencies of
> republican government may be retained and its im-
> perfections lessened or avoided.

A new government that wishes to disperse power must draw up a constitutional document indicating which agencies are permitted to perform which functions. An established society, such as Great Britain, may develop such procedures over a long period of time and without a written constitution. However, the American states had not had several centuries during which they could experiment by trial and error. They were confronted with immediate problems which required an immediate solution.

THE SEPARATION OF POWERS   The new national government would not, then, be a monolithic structure. Hamilton and Madison both empha- sized the fact that the proposed constitution made explicit provision for three separate departments. If such a trifurcation was not the most conducive to efficiency, it was nevertheless necessary if the freedoms of citizens and the identities of states were to be protected. "No politi- cal truth is certainly of greater intrinsic value, or is stamped with the authority of more enlightened patrons of liberty," Madison wrote in No. 47, "than that . . . the accumulation of all powers, legislative, executive, and judiciary, in the same hands, whether of one, a few, or many, and whether hereditary, self-appointed, or elective, may justly be pronounced the very definition of tyranny."

The idea that powers can be separated is a principle of government rather than an explicit guide to practice. Indeed, three different inter- pretations can be given to the separation of powers theory.

1. Separation of powers means, first of all, that a single individual will not serve in more than one branch of the government at any given time. The theory is that one set of *men* will administer the laws, and that another set of men will enact them. A legislator, for example, should not be able to ascend to the judicial bench to interpret a statute that he earlier participated in drafting. But even the proposed con- stitution had at least one exception to this rule: the Vice President, a member of the executive branch, would preside over the Senate and would have a vote there in case of a tie.

2. The next meaning of separation of powers is that the legislative, executive, and judicial *functions* are different and that they should

be performed by the three independent branches. Making laws, administering laws, and interpreting laws are separate processes and whatever overlap there is among them can and should be held to a minimum. The Constitution, for example, forbade the Congress from passing bills of attainder; for the punishment of individual citizens is a judicial function.

3. And, finally, the principle goes on to assert that each branch should have some *check* over the operations of the others. The jurisdiction of any one department must be sufficiently broad so that it can, as occasion demands, veto the acts of its coequal departments. Such a veto need not be permanent or final, and it need not be applicable in all circumstances. Sometimes it will serve as a delaying action, forcing a department to reconsider the wisdom of a measure it may have enacted in haste. At other times a veto will be a potential weapon and thus one branch will, in fear or anticipation, temper its behavior lest it be checked by another. Indeed, the potentiality of checks and balances probably has more day-to-day effectiveness than their actual use. For politicians have a tendency to anticipate sanctions and thus act in ways that will make the actual employment of those sanctions unnecessary.

The theory of mutual checks and balances can best be understood if one thinks of a triangle with six arrows skirting its three borders, as shown on the diagram. Each arrow represents the one or more checks that one branch has over another. Some of these checks come readily to mind: the President's veto of acts of Congress, congressional approval of executive appointees, the Supreme Court's review of administration rules and regulations. Others are less obvious: congressional modification and repassage of a law to circumvent an earlier

The theory of mutual checks and balances

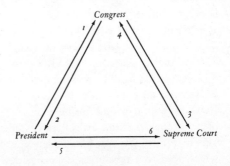

Supreme Court decision; or the President's refusal to spend money that Congress has appropriated for a particular purpose. A student of American government should be able to "fill in the arrows" in some detail and be able to describe the wide variety of checks that are available to the various departments. At the same time he must understand that some are more important than others, that some are used frequently and others hardly at all.

PARCHMENT AND PRACTICE   Madison was quick to admit that any application of the principle of separation of powers would be beset with practical difficulties. In No. 37 he acknowledged that the science of politics has yet to find a way of encasing men and functions in airtight compartments:

> Experience has instructed us that no skill in the science of government has yet been able to discriminate and define, with sufficient certainty, its three great provinces—the legislative, executive, and judiciary; or even the privileges and powers of the different legislative branches. Questions daily occur in the course of practice which prove the obscurity which reigns in these subjects, and which puzzle the greatest adepts in political science.

Indeed, the whole notion of dispersing power among several governmental departments did not come from any treatise in political theory, but was rather derived from the political experience of the states and before them the colonies. From Georgia to New Hampshire, from the time of the establishment of the earliest colonial legislature, there had been various attempts to separate the major functions of government into discrete agencies. Yet none of the states or colonies provided a perfect illustration of the principle. In No. 47 Madison surveyed the experience of all 13 states and concluded: "There is not a single instance in which the several departments of power have been kept absolutely separate and distinct."

A written constitution had to operate within practical considerations. The separation of powers, accompanied by checks and balances, would be written into the basic law as a curb on the national government. But that in itself would not be enough. "A mere demarcation on parchment of the constitutional limits of the several departments," Madison said in No. 48, "is not a sufficient guard against those encroachments which lead to a tyrannical concentration of all the powers of government in the same hands." Other extraconstitutional protections—in No. 51 he called them "auxiliary precautions"—would be needed. And these, as will be seen, would be found not in a parchment document but in the very structure of American society itself.

A REPRESENTATIVE CONSTITUTION

A DEMOCRACY OR A REPUBLIC? To the minds of the *Federalist* authors democracy was something to be feared. For to them it conveyed the idea of direct self-government on the part of the people. In its least objectionable form it would mean local government by a town meeting where the whole adult population of a community would participate in making policy. At the other extreme it would involve enacting national legislation by popular referendum. The *Federalist* authors' distrust of democracy was based on their theory of human nature. For if citizens are fundamentally intemperate and irrational, especially when they assemble, then the laws they enact will corrupt the true ends of government. For Hamilton and Madison, then, "democracy" was construed as "popular democracy," even "populist democracy."

Although the town meeting has ceased to be an important institution, and referendums are confined to the state and local levels, the *Federalist* conception of democracy continues to have relevance in American politics. What it stands for, in essence, is an attitude of mind on the part of ordinary citizens. The people in a popular democracy will continually be preoccupied with governmental policy, and they will form and express their opinions without stopping to ask if they are competent to do so. Elected politicians, under such circumstances, are forced to heed the momentary whims of their constituents or else they will be punished at the next election. Democratic citizens, then, do not simply elect their rulers. Indeed, the *Federalist* authors had no objection to that. What characterizes the citizens of a democracy is that *between* elections they continue to voice their political sentiments and to gain an undue influence over the men they elected to public office. While this conception of democracy may be a caricature, it must be remembered that fear gives rise to a gross exaggeration of reality. And Hamilton and Madison were haunted by the fear of a public that would be overinterested in the affairs of government, obtrusive in their behavior, and arrogant in their demeanor.

THE DEFERENTIAL VOTER The proposed constitution, therefore, was not intended to be a democratic instrument. Citizens were to have the vote, but once Election Day was over the business of government was to remain in the hands of the elected representatives. This "republican"—as opposed to "democratic"—arrangement, Madison wrote in No. 10, was designed "to refine and enlarge the public views by passing them through the medium of a chosen body of citizens, whose wisdom may best discern the true interest of their country and whose patriotism and love of justice will be least likely to sacrifice it to temporary or partial considerations." This suggests that there do exist in society at least *some* men who are superior to others in regard to wisdom, patriotism, and love of justice. For all their generalizations about the parlous state of the human condition, Hamilton and Madison were nevertheless to rely heavily on the expectation that men of superior qualities would rise to positions of power in the governmental system.

How was this to occur? The *Federalist* authors held to the hope that the average voter would, when elections were held, defer to men of greater attainments than his own. Rather than looking for a candidate coming from his own class or occupation, the ordinary citizen would vote for someone he acknowledged to be his better. In No. 35 Hamilton asserted that "mechanics and manufacturers"—that is, skilled and unskilled workers—would have the good sense to elect businessmen rather than people from their own station in life:

> Mechanics and manufacturers will always be inclined, with few exceptions, to give their votes to merchants in preference to persons of their own professions or trades. Those discerning citizens are well aware . . . that the merchant is their natural patron and friend; and they are aware that however great the confidence they may justly feel in their own good sense, their interests can be more effectually promoted by the merchant than by themselves. They are sensible that their habits in life have not been such as to give them those acquired endowments, without which in a deliberative assembly the greatest natural abilities are for the most part useless. . . .

Whether this statement is a prediction of what *will* happen or an expression of a hope about what *ought* to happen is difficult to say. In one sense Hamilton was suggesting that the ordinary voters would defer to citizens of superior attainments. In another there is the impression that Hamilton is exhorting the skilled and unskilled workers among his readers to adopt humility in their voting behavior and to display a measure of deference when they go to the polls.

THE DEFERENTIAL CANDIDATE   Habits of deference would have to be engendered if the republican principle was to be established. On the one hand rulers were to be elected either directly or indirectly, and it was hoped that they would be the most capable men in society. "The aim of every political constitution is, or ought to be, first to obtain for rulers men who possess most wisdom to discern, and most virtue to pursue, the common good of the society," Madison said in No. 57. And then later on the same page he stated that the franchise, the instrument for deciding who will govern, will be universally extended:

> Who are to be the electors of [i.e., voters for] the federal representatives? Not the rich, more than the poor; not the learned, more than the ignorant; not the haughty heirs of distinguished names, more than the humble sons of obscurity and unpropitious fortune. The electors are to be the great body of the people of the United States.

Hamilton and Madison believed that universality of suffrage and superiority of representation could be reconciled if the elected lawmakers took pains to keep in touch with the needs of their constituents. While a legislator might not come from the same class as the people in his district, he could nevertheless acquaint himself with their sentiments and interests. "Is it not natural that a man who is a candidate for the favor of the people . . . should take care to inform himself of their dispositions and inclinations and should be willing to allow them their proper degree of influence upon his conduct?" Hamilton asked in No. 35. Madison answered this question in No. 57 by pointing to the elements which would link representatives and constituents: "Duty, gratitude, interest, ambition itself, are the cords by which they will be bound to fidelity and sympathy with the great mass of the people." It is interesting to note how certain themes recur in this analysis. Hamilton took pains to point out that voters should exert no more than their "proper degree of influence" upon their representatives, that they should forebear from interfering in affairs that are best left to those who are able to take a long-range view. And Madison went on to state that while elected lawmakers may be superior men, they also possess the less praiseworthy qualities of interest and ambition, and these will keep them attentive to the needs of those with the power to elect them to office. In this way, then, the republican basis of a "parchment constitution" is underpinned by traits of human behavior which might otherwise serve less noble purposes. In other words, a system of government must not try to abolish interests and emotions but must rather channel them so that they serve the national welfare.

THE PURPOSES OF POLITICS

POWER: NATIONAL AND INTERNATIONAL The assumption of the *Federalist* authors was that before self-government is possible it is necessary to have a government, that political authority must be established before individual liberty can be secured. This is why *The Federalist* does not constitute a treatise on democracy; it is why it always discusses freedom in the context of social order. The men who drafted the proposed constitution were persuaded that the national government needed to be strong, and this conviction was founded on real fears. There was not only the threat of conflict between the states but also of insurrection within the states. The memory of Shays' Rebellion in Massachusetts was still fresh; and the tensions between states over title to what were then considered western lands were causes for concern. The specter of European power rose across the Atlantic, and not a few of these nations ringed the new America with their colonies in the Western Hemisphere. Added to this was the frequency of Indian wars and the intensity of commercial competition. All these were real threats and they could only be checked if national power was created to meet the challenge. "I acknowledge my aversion to every project that is calculated to disarm the government of a single weapon, which in any possible contingency might be usefully employed for the general defense and security," Hamilton wrote in No. 36.

Hamilton's concern over creating a strong nation was not a little infused with patriotism of his own. He was a proud American and it was his fervent desire to demonstrate to the countries of Europe that the new republic would more than hold its own in the arena of world affairs. In No. 11 he allowed his emotions to flow freely:

> Europe, by her arms and by her negotiations, by force and by fraud, has in different degrees extended her dominion . . . Africa, Asia, and America

have successively felt her domination. The superiority she has long maintained has tempted her to plume herself as mistress of the world, and to consider the rest of mankind as created for her benefit. Men admired as profound philosophers have in direct terms attributed to her inhabitants a physical superiority and have gravely asserted that all animals, and with them the human species, degenerate in America—that even dogs cease to bark after having breathed awhile in our atmosphere. Facts have too long supported these arrogant pretensions of the European. It belongs to us to vindicate the honor of the human race, and to teach that assuming brother moderation. Union will enable us to do it. Disunion will add another victim to his triumphs. Let Americans disdain to be the instruments of European greatness!

The emotion of national pride invariably accompanies political realism as a new country seeks to establish itself. The patronizing manner of the Europeans rankled American sensibilities; Hamilton sought to show that the United States could stand up against England, France, and Spain if it were willing to create a central government with the power to act purposively.

Yet the emphasis was not solely on military strength. National power, to Hamilton's mind, had to be used to create a viable economy. Commerce and industry had to be encouraged; and a stable business community for investors, both domestic and foreign, had to be maintained. The mercantile acts which Britain had imposed on the colonies had stifled economic growth. It was Hamilton's vision that it was the role of government to give capitalism every possible stimulus; and later, as Secretary of the Treasury, he proposed a wide variety of policies to encourage the emerging entrepreneurs. "Under a vigorous national government," he said in No. 11, "the natural strength and resources of the country, directed to a common interest, would baffle all the combinations of European jealousy to restrain our growth." But governmental support of trade and manufacturing was not simply designed to tweak the nose of Europe. On the contrary, Hamilton continued, "an active commerce, an extensive navigation, and a flourishing marine would then be the inevitable offspring of moral and physical necessity."

The positive purpose was to build a nation by founding it on an industrialized economy. American capitalism would develop only if a vigorous government gave its authoritative support to the business community. In putting this idea forward Hamilton was not only foreseeing the future; he was also serving to shape the future of American life.

Turning to the domestic scene Hamilton saw no less reason for securing national power. While others might talk of the importance of individual freedom, minority rights, and local autonomy, Hamilton spoke of the threat of factionalism, rebellion, and license. To him the several states were so many seedbeds of disruption and disorder. Had not Shays' uprising in Massachusetts been but the latest of many recent challenges to authority? If Europe was to be kept at bay and if productive property was to be safeguarded at home, then national political authority had to be centralized. To drive home this lesson Hamilton cited the experience of history, and warned his readers that what had happened in the past could well happen again. In No. 9 he wrote:

> A firm union will be of the utmost moment to the peace and liberty of the states as a barrier against domestic faction and insurrection. It is impossible to read the history of the petty republics of Greece and Italy without feeling sensations of horror and disgust at the distractions with which they were continually agitated, and at the rapid succession of revolutions by which they were kept in a state of perpetual vibration between the extremes of tyranny and anarchy.

If events made it necessary, government power might even express itself in the form of marching into a state or locality and putting down those groups of citizens who refused to obey national law. He was later to use national power in just this way to deal with the Whisky Rebellion in Pennsylvania, for it was clear that to him political authority was meaningless if it did not have the ability to compel.

MADISON'S DILEMMA In this part of the discussion Madison tended to remain silent. This was not because he disagreed with his coauthor but was rather due to desire to reconcile opposing political principles. Madison, too, was worried about domestic factionalism, and he knew full well that divergent interests could injure the public well-being as they pursued their selfish ends. "The regulation of these various and interfering interests forms the principal task of modern legislation," he said in No. 10; and the exercise of such regulation "involves the spirit of party and faction in the necessary and ordinary operations of the government." But Madison, as will be seen shortly, wanted it both ways. If he acknowledged that political power must be used to regulate the activities of groups in the society, he also wanted those groups to have a positive role in making governmental policy. In other words, groups must not only be regulated—they must also be represented in the government of the republic. In No. 37 he reminded his readers that such a reconciliation had been intended by the men who drew up the Constitution. "Among the difficulties encountered by the convention," he said, "a very important one must have lain in combining the requisite stability and energy in government with the inviolable attention due to liberty and the republican form."

The tensions between authority and liberty, between regulation and representation, are continually present. Hamilton was most concerned to effect the consolidation of national power as a first step, and he was often impatient with those who demanded guarantees of freedom against an allegedly oppressive government. At the same time he wanted to protect the liberty of at least one group in society—the businessmen —and he proposed that public agencies bend every effort to extend the freedom of the men charged with developing the economy. As for those lacking in wealth or in ambition—which is to say the majority of Americans—Hamilton was distinctly unimpressed with whatever claims they might make for political attention. Indeed, he suspected that pandering to majority sentiment would jeopardize the freedoms of the minority that really counted. The politician who takes seriously the whims and wishes of the general public is a dangerous man. "Of those men who have overturned the liberties of republics," he wrote in No. 1, "the greatest number have begun their careers by paying obsequious court to the people, commencing demagogues and ending tyrants."

Madison was never so harsh when he spoke of the common man and he was slower to denigrate popular leaders. Nevertheless, he was a republican rather than a democrat, according to his understanding of those terms, and he was wary of untempered majority rule. Where he parted company with Hamilton was in his solutions to problems that the two men agreed had to be solved. Whereas Hamilton stressed the vigorous use of national power, Madison reemphasized constitutional checks. One reason for this difference in approach may be suggested.

Both *Federalist* authors wanted America to be a free society. However, the question arises: Freedom for whom? Hamilton wanted to protect the freedom of businessmen and others who would contribute to the growth of the nation's economy. This group, he felt, must be safeguarded from tyranny at the hands of a jealous and underprivileged majority. Madison, on the other hand, wanted to guarantee the rights of a rather different minority. He was concerned about freedom of expression: the liberty to speak, assemble, and worship as one pleased. And constitutional provisions would not suffice as a defense of these freedoms. Something more was needed, and therefore Madison looked to the basic structure of American society for his answer.

Review Questions

1. What is the *Federalist* theory of human nature?

2. What is the value of basing a government on a written constitution?

3. What is the separation of powers designed to achieve?

4. Why did the *Federalist* authors fear democracy?

5. In what spheres did Hamilton advocate a strenuous government?

6. Did Madison accept Hamilton's ideas on national power?

FEDERAL GOVERNMENT AND SOCIAL PLURALISM

Chapter 6

The thirteen states, as British colonies, all had separate identities for many years prior to the Revolution. They were, therefore, communities in their own right and each had a history and a local pride of its own. In order to secure even rudimentary agreement on the proposed constitution the *Federalist* authors had to persuade their readers that all the states would retain significant power in local matters. Hamilton and Madison were well aware of the strength of the opposition to the Constitution. In No. 1 Hamilton frankly acknowledged that certain interests in the states would be harmed upon the creation of a national government. "Among the most formidable of the obstacles which the new constitution will have to encounter," he wrote, "may readily be distinguished the obvious interest of a certain class of men in every state to resist all changes which may hazard a diminution of power, emolument, and consequence of the offices they hold under the state establishments." Not simply officeholders, but hundreds of thousands of ordinary citizens with strong loyalties to the states had to be convinced that their freedoms would not be abridged. This task of persuasion fell to Madison.

In seven papers, beginning with No. 39, Madison sought to demonstrate that political power in America would be shared between the state and national governments, and that the authority granted to the national government was the minimum necessary for America's survival. Madison continually alluded to the doctrine of constitutionalism, for only with a written document would the limits on national power be demarcated and the extent of state powers be guaranteed. In other words, a federal system is only possible if the bounds of the national and state jurisdictions are specified in a constitutional document. Without such an aid there would be constant quarrels—not only about substantive issues of power and policy but also about which agencies were legitimately entitled to settle those quarrels. Madison sought to satisfy both the proponents of centralization and states' rights by taking a middle road. In No. 39 he said: "The proposed constitution, therefore, is, in strictness, neither a national nor a federal constitution, but a composition of both."

FEDERALISM AND FREEDOM The chief worry of the states' rights advocates was that the power that would be centralized in the national government would be used to tyrannize the various regions and localities throughout the country. Local customs and regional interests might be ignored and even injured if political authority gravitated to the center. The principle of federalism, therefore, was created to ensure that substantial power would remain in the separate states. And to this was added the principle of separation of powers, in an attempt to ensure that even the national government itself would not be monolithic in structure.

It is clear that the states' rights proponents were not the only ones who were anxious about centralized power. Even those who were sympathetic to the idea of national authority were concerned lest the legislative and perhaps other branches of the new government be captured by the wrong people. There was, in short, the fear of majority tyranny: the fear that with universal suffrage and widespread political participation the masses would take over and endanger the interests of certain individuals in society. Madison sought to allay these anxieties, and in the course of doing this he found it necessary to present a full-scale analysis of the social structure that would underpin the American political system.

CLASSES, INTERESTS, PARTIES

American society, Madison said in No. 10, had been and would continue to be diversified and heterogeneous. The larger the collection of individuals the more will one encounter unequal drives, talents and ambitions. Variations in intelligence, energy, and aspiration are to be observed among the members of a population. This variety brings in its wake important consequences that are social and psychological. To begin with, many interests will emerge in the society, and these will result in differences of opinion on the part of the individuals who hold them. Because the reason of man is an imperfect instrument, citizens tend to be myopic, wrongly confusing their own interests with the common good. As each person is anxious to promote his own well-being, the political opinions in society are distorted in their perception of reality and divisive in their impact. Of all the interests that blind the intelligence and promote conflict, Madison said, property is the most important. On this basis Madison links together his theory of human nature with a theory of society:

> As long as the reason of man continues fallible, and he is at liberty to exercise it, different opinions will be formed. As long as the connection subsists between his reason and his self-love, his opinions and his passions will have a reciprocal influence on each other; and the former will be objects to which the latter will attach themselves. The diversity in the faculties of men, from which the rights of property originate, is not less an insuperable obstacle to the uniformity of interests. The protection of these faculties is the first object of government. From the protection of different and unequal faculties of acquiring property, the possession of different degrees and kinds of property immediately results; and

> from the influence of these on the sentiments and
> views of the respective proprietors ensues a divi-
> sion of the society into different interests and parties.

This passage, like all the passages in No. 10, calls for close reading.
Madison is saying that human potentialities must be given the opportunity to express themselves, and that it is the responsibility of government in a free society to encourage such expression. Yet if government carries out this obligation, then vigorous and talented individuals
will inevitably acquire property and develop interests of their own. The
possession of these interests will obscure their perception of the common good and will distort their political opinions. In other words, by
encouraging self-expression and property ownership the government
also encourages social disharmony and human irrationality. If individual
development and material success are blessings worth having, it must
also be understood that they are to be had at a cost. Society will be
less harmonious and the opinions and behavior of individuals will be
less realistic. Madison settled for this outcome, knowing it was the
price to be paid for individualism.

POWER AND PROPERTY   American society, then, would be composed of
many interests and groups. All of them would pursue goals of their own;
and none of them, despite their protestations to the contrary, would promote the general welfare. These groups—Madison called them "factions"
—present a challenge to government because they accentuate whatever
differences there are in society and they necessarily compete for power
with their own interests in mind. Again in No. 10 Madison elaborated
his theory and it deserves to be quoted in full:

> The latent causes of faction are thus sown in the
> nature of man; and we see them everywhere brought
> into different degrees of activity, according to the
> different circumstances of civil society. A zeal for dif-
> ferent opinions concerning religion, concerning gov-
> ernment, and many other points, as well of specu-
> lation as of practice; an attachment to different
> leaders ambitiously contending for pre-eminence and
> power; or to persons of other descriptions whose
> fortunes have been interesting to the human pas-
> sions, have, in turn, divided mankind into parties,
> inflamed them with mutual animosity, and rendered

them much more disposed to vex and oppress each other than to co-operate for their common good.

So strong is this propensity of mankind to fall into mutual animosities that where no substantial occasion presents itself the most frivolous and fanciful distinctions have been sufficient to kindle their unfriendly passions and excite their most violent conflicts.

But the most common and durable source of factions has been the various and unequal distribution of property. Those who hold and those who are without property have ever formed distinct interests in society. Those who are creditors and those who are debtors, fall under a like discrimination. A landed interest, a manufacturing interest, a mercantile interest, a moneyed interest, with many lesser interests, grow up of necessity in civilized nations, and divide them into different classes, actuated by different sentiments and views.

The regulation of these various and interfering interests forms the principal task of modern legislation and involves the spirit of party and faction in the necessary and ordinary operations of the government.

VERTICAL VERSUS HORIZONTAL INTERESTS The "most common and durable" source of division in society, Madison said, must be attributed to property ownership. The propertied and the propertyless classes are the two most significant groups, and any analysis of social conflict must begin with the tensions between them. However, Madison's framework does not end at this point. In addition to these two main classes, there are many interests in society. Madison's meaning may best be understood by contrasting a "horizontal" division, representing the propertied and propertyless classes, against the various "vertical" divisions, representing the disparate interests within the two major classes.

The diagram shows that where there is a division *between* the propertied and propertyless classes, there are also subdivisions—and hence disagreements—*within* the two classes. Property owners who are creditors will often be in conflict with property owners who are debtors; manufacturers will not always agree with financiers. At the same time,

Creditor interest	Creditor interest
Debtor interest	Debtor interest
Landed interest	Landed interest
Mercantile interest	Mercantile interest
Manufacturing interest	Manufacturing interest
Financial interest	Financial interest
"Lesser" interests	"Lesser" interests
PROPERTYLESS CLASS	PROPERTIED CLASS

Classes and interests

there will frequently be a sense of fellow feeling among the members of the two classes *within* an interest. Thus, while the propertyless class is in the majority, the people who comprise it are by no means single-minded in their interests.

This depiction of society lessens the possibility that the propertyless majority will use its power to tyrannize those who own property. As Hamilton pointed out in his discussion of voting behavior, there is reason to believe that individuals employed in farming or commerce or manufacturing will identify their own interests with those of their employers and will allow members of the propertied class to represent them. Thus, both the bank owner and the bank clerk, one a man of property and the other not, belong to the "financial interest" and will often stand together against competing interests.

Furthermore, Madison granted that while property might be the most common and durable source of political division, he also pointed out that "many lesser interests" grow up. And by these he clearly meant religious interests, ethnic interests, regional interests, and ideological interests. While these, to his mind, might be of lesser importance they did play a role in politics and often a key one. Finally, Madison saw it as government's role to regulate interests as well as to represent them. The state, for Madison, was to stand apart from and serve as a control over the activities of interests and groups. This meant that the government would have a source of power and goals that were independent of any one class or interest.

THE SIZE OF SOCIETY   The thirteen states had a population of approximately 3 million, and in terms of size alone it was clear that the United States would be a large country. To the members of minority groups who were worrying about possible majority tyranny under the proposed constitution, Madison pointed out that the very size of the new nation would go far toward dampening this threat. "The greater number of citizens and extent of territory," he said in No. 10, will be the "circumstance principally which renders factious combinations less to be dreaded." There might be great hordes of propertyless workers in Massachusetts and New York; but as individuals they would also have diverse regional, occupational, and religious loyalties and it seemed highly unlikely that they would combine across state boundaries to organize a single "working-class" party.

This is why Madison favored a nation that would cover a large territory. "Extend the sphere and you take in a greater variety of parties and interests," he continued in No. 10. "You make it less probable that a majority of the whole will have a common motive to invade the rights of other citizens." A further consequence would be to localize any tendency toward majority tyranny. The propertyless class might ascend to power in the state governments of Georgia or Pennsylvania, but it would be improbable that such a revolution would contaminate neighboring states or the country as a whole. Madison concluded No. 10 by predicting that "the influence of factious leaders may kindle a flame within their particular states but will be unable to spread a general conflagration through the other states."

POLITICS WITHOUT PARTIES   Neither Hamilton nor Madison approved of political parties. Factions, classes, and interests were seen as the necessary accompaniments of a free society, but they were a challenge rather than a blessing. If political groupings were to be based on property or other interests, it was to be hoped that they would confine their activities to localities and to promoting specific policies rather than comprehensive programs. The idea that factions might organize as political parties and run candidates for public office was something that the *Federalist* authors preferred not to consider. To their minds there was sufficient disharmony in society without building those tensions into the political system. As far as Hamilton and Madison could see, individual candidates would present themselves for election; there would be no party labels and no slates of nominees. In this way voters would cast their ballots in their role as *citizens* rather than on the basis of special interests they might have. Furthermore, candidates would be

THE STUDY OF POLITICS **82**

judged on their merits and they would have to make a broad appeal to a large and diversified electorate in their constituencies. Above all, the *Federalist* authors wanted to avoid national parties—parties that would coalesce the interests within various states into centralized organizations. For all their concern to establish a national government they were unwilling to espouse parties drawn on similar lines. The reason for this was that Hamilton and Madison, no less than many of their readers, were fearful of the rise of a majority party that would trample on the rights and liberties of minorities. "When a majority is included in a faction," Madison wrote in No. 10, "the form of popular government . . . enables it to sacrifice to its ruling passion or interest both the public good and the rights of their citizens." National parties, especially if one of them attracted a majority of Americans to its banner, would do much to bring about just this result.

THE SOCIOLOGY OF FREEDOM

In No. 51 Madison continued to relate his theories of human nature and social structure to his view of political liberty. In permitting universal suffrage and representative institutions, the framers of the constitution granted that government was to be based on the consent of the governed. This meant that politics would be a reflection of society, that the interests and aspirations of social interests and classes would contribute to shaping the political system. It was for that reason that Madison, in No. 10, devoted so much attention to his sociological analysis. With this task accomplished, he was ready to turn to the problem of human freedom. How can minority rights be reconciled with majority rule? To speak thus of "majority rule" is to make the assumption that a permanent and homogeneous "majority" will emerge to monopolize political power. On the contrary, Madison asserted in No. 51, there is reason to believe that this will not be the path of development in America:

> Whilst all authority in it will be derived from and dependent on the society, the society itself will be broken into so many parts, interests and classes of citizens, that the rights of individuals, or of the minority, will be in little danger from interested combinations of the majority. In a free government the security for civil rights must be the same as that for religious rights. It consists in the one case

in the multiplicity of interests, and in the other in the multiplicity of sects. The degree of security in both cases will depend on the number of interests and sects; and this may be presumed to depend on the extent of country and number of people comprehended under the same government.

The American "majority," in other words, will be a shifting coalition of groups. Its composition in terms of the people who belong to it, will alter from time to time and from issue to issue. A citizen may find himself on the majority side one day but on the next he will be among the dissenters. While part of the time every individual may have to abide by majority dictates that he finds disagreeable, there is little likelihood that the members of any one group in society will suffer sustained and uninterrupted oppression.

INTERESTS: INDIVIDUAL AND SOCIAL   The "multiplicity of interests" that Madison spoke of must be construed at two levels: the individual and the social. In the former case each citizen will himself have several interests he wishes to promote. In the latter case society as a whole will be composed of various interests, each attracting the loyalties of groups of citizens.

On the individual level it can be suggested that each American will have a religious interest, an occupational interest, and various others. One citizen may, for example, be: (1) a bank clerk; (2) a Methodist; (3) a Southerner; (4) a member of the white race; (5) an opera-goer; and (6) of military age. In all these "roles" he will have political opinions, ranging from government control over liquor sales to government support for opera. In some of his roles, as when he is white and a Protestant, he will be in the majority. This citizen, then, shifts from majority to minority status as different issues arise. In his majority role as a white man he may, wittingly or unwittingly, serve to tyrannize nonwhites who are a minority in the community. In his minority role as an opera-lover he may feel himself oppressed by the philistine majority, the members of which prefer television Westerns to higher art forms and who do not want to see their taxes going to subsidize Wagner and Mozart. Madison's assumption was that all Americans would possess a variety of interests, economic and non-economic, and that they would consequently play several roles in the political drama. Were citizens to have but a single interest, and were this interest to be their property ownership or lack of it, then there would indeed be the danger of a permanent and continually victimized minority in society.

In terms of society, Madison said that the social whole would be "broken into so many parts, interests, and classes of citizens." No single part or interest or class would contain a majority of citizens; if a majority were formed on any issue, it would simply consist of a transient coalition of groups. For example, there is a Protestant majority in America, and it may be inquired why its representatives do not enact legislation penalizing the Catholic minority in the country. Madison's answer was not that the Protestants are notably tolerant nor was it that they believe in religious liberty for all. The answer was that the Protestant majority is itself a coalition of Baptists, Methodists, Episcopalians, Presbyterians, and Lutherans. Each of these denominations had had its own history of persecution when it was in the minority, and therefore all of them agree to tolerate other religions—including the Catholics—for fear that they may at some future time be subjected to majority oppression. Furthermore, the members of the Protestant coalition are not all of the belief that Catholics ought to be penalized, and were that issue even to be raised there would be every chance that the Protestant coalition would fall apart. In a pluralistic society toleration becomes the operative rule in the political game. Respect for the freedom of others is the price paid for having one's own freedom left intact. Political liberty is guaranteed not so much by a constitution—which is, after all, a "demarcation on parchment"—as it is a product of the toleration that groups impose on themselves.

CONFLICT AND THE GENERAL GOOD   Madison ended No. 51 by assuring his readers that majority tyranny lay more in their imaginations than in the American reality:

> In the extended republic of the United States, and among the great variety of interests, parties, and sects which it embraces, a coalition of a majority of the whole society could seldom take place on any other principles than those of justice and the general good; whilst there being thus less danger to a minority from the will of a major party, there must be less pretext, also, to provide for the security of the former, by introducing into the government a

> will not dependent on the latter, or, in other words,
> a will independent of the society itself.

The kinds of policies that will muster the support of coalition-type majorities will, in all likelihood, promote the public welfare.

On first reading this proposition of Madison's runs directly counter to Hamilton's view, stated in No. 6, that "momentary passions and immediate interests have a more active and imperious control over human conduct than general or remote considerations of policy, utility, or justice." How does one square the *Federalist* conception of human nature, as expressed here by Hamilton, with Madison's contention that justice and political freedom may ultimately be secured via the group struggle? The answer is that these ends are achieved not *because* of human nature but *in spite of* it. Individuals and groups are passionate and self-interested, Madison would certainly grant, but out of their clashes in the political arena must emerge compromises. Freedom and justice are not attained because rational men consciously pursue those goals. Human reason is too imperfect and human perversity is too pervasive to allow for that. On the contrary, the public good is an unanticipated by-product of group conflict; the general welfare develops out of the collisions of particular interests and it is expressed in compromises where all parties are partially satisfied but where none are entirely contented.

Madison seemed to prefer having a "neutral" government, for he was uneasy about the creation of "a will independent of the society itself." He was concerned lest political authority become a power apart from the individuals and groups who comprise the society. For history had amply demonstrated that agencies of government are apt to fall into the hands of men who use them to promote interests detrimental to the general welfare. A government with a will of its own, a government that is impervious to the needs of the interests that make up society, can be just as tyrannical as one based on popular consent.

Yet Madison was not able to be entirely consistent in this area. In speaking of the group struggle, he said in No. 10, "the regulation of these various and interfering interests forms the principal task of modern legislation." Yet if government is to regulate groups in society by means of legislation, then the power behind that legislation must clearly emanate from a "will independent of society." The point, of course, is that neither principle—government as representative versus government as regulator—must be carried to an extreme. Government must be responsive to the expressed will of the people, but it must also have a will of its own. Hamilton stressed the latter case and there were times, especially in No. 10, when Madison supported him. On other occasions, particularly in No. 51, Madison expressed fears of a too strenuous government. Madison's two minds express an enduring dilemma in political life. If government is too indulgent in catering to the demands of interest groups, then it may not be able to fashion policies that will serve the interests of the nation as a whole. But a strong and purposeful government may exceed its mandate and commit the country to courses of action it will later regret. Unfortunately it is evading the issue to say that these two outlooks should be "balanced." What must be achieved is an understanding of how the regulation of interests rather than their representation affects different groups in society. Those who fear and those who welcome governmental activity in a particular sphere usually have different conceptions of what makes for individual freedom and the good life. What appears to be "regulation" to the eyes of some groups looks like "representation" to others. Behind the argument over supposedly abstract principles, then, lies not so much a conflict of ideas as of interests. This, in sum, is the Madisonian lesson.

THE ISOLATED DISSENTER   There remains one area where governmental power must necessarily operate independent of group power. In No. 51 Madison expressed concern for both "the rights of individuals or of the minority." Most minority interests, as has been pointed out, can fend for themselves. Farmers and bank clerks, Negroes and Catholics, veterans and retired people—all these minority groups are capable of organizing their members, forming alliances with other groups, and influencing the course of public policy. However, there are many isolated individuals in society who do not belong to groups in any meaningful sense of that term and yet who need political protection if they are to exercise their rights of expression. Various examples may be cited: (1) a citizen who does not belong to a recognized religious sect but who wishes to be exempted from military service on conscientious grounds; (2) a housewife who disapproves of the local public schools and who wishes to educate her children at home; (3) a union member who does not want the money he pays in dues used for political purposes. All these are isolated individuals, and they are not represented in the give and take of the group struggle. Their freedoms can be abridged by private organizations like a trade union, by a local authority such as a school board, or by an agency of the national government. The rights of individuals—as distinct from groups—can only be protected if some department of the government intervenes and exercises power on their behalf. The courts are most frequently called on to perform this function, as the administration and the legislature are rarely willing to act in this capacity. In all such cases the government is expressing a will of its own—a will to preserve individual liberty—rather than representing group interests. Indeed, in most instances of this kind the government will find itself acting in defiance of the majority of citizens, for the American people tend to be rather impatient about the eccentricities of isolated dissenters. The conclusion must be that Madison's sociology of freedom serves to protect groups rather than individuals. In the latter instance the heretic and the dissenter must call on the courts, as an independent arm of the government, to protect him from victimization by groups and institutions in the community. Whether there will be a sympathetic response to this call is a difficult problem and it permits of no easy answer. It was, at all events, a problem that the *Federalist* authors chose not to discuss.

Review Questions

1. How does federalism protect freedom?

2. What are "factions" and why was Madison fearful of them?

3. Why is it important that society be broken into "many parts, interests, and classes"?

4. Is the threat of majority tyranny a real or an imaginary danger?

5. What is the role of government in relation to group conflict?

6. How are the rights of isolated individuals to be protected?

INSTITUTIONS OF GOVERNMENT

Chapter 7

As they discussed the powers and functions of the major branches of the national government the *Federalist* authors were compelled to make predictions about how these institutions would operate in the future. Prediction, especially in the political realm, is always a risky enterprise. How can the drafters of a constitution foresee the ways in which governmental practice will develop over subsequent decades? The important point is that Hamilton and Madison made so many penetrating forecasts. To be sure, they were often wrong in their judgments, but it is too much to ask mortal men to be always correct in prophesying what will take place in the century and a half after their time. Who among us can say what the government of the United States will look like in the year 2110?

THE CONGRESS

By the standards that prevailed at the time of the writing of *The Federalist*, the House of Representatives was to be a large body. Its initial membership, upon ratification of the Constitution, was to stand at 65. In contrast, there would be only 26 senators. In No. 58 Madison suggested that the House of Representatives would be more powerful than the Senate; and this would be so because the members of the House, taken together, would represent a majority of the electorate. That is, the votes in each separate district that elected the representatives to office would add up to a national majority, thus providing that chamber with a powerful constituency of countrywide proportions. In this connection Madison wrote in No. 58:

> Notwithstanding the equal authority which will subsist between the two houses on all legislative subjects . . . it cannot be doubted that the House, composed of the greater number of members, when supported by the more powerful states, and speaking the known and determined sense of a majority of people, will have no small advantage in a question depending on the comparative firmness of the two houses.

The House of Representatives, then, would be susceptible to democratic pressures. It would be likely to carry out the wishes of the majority of the American people without questioning the wisdom of these mandates. This would be so because Representatives would have only two-year terms and would have to be sensitive to the demands of their constituents if they were to continue in office. Furthermore, the more populous states would swing substantial weight, perhaps wielding their power by means of "bloc" voting on legislation. If there was one institution in the new government that caused unease in the minds of the *Federalist* authors it was plainly the House of Representatives. As early as in No. 6 Hamilton asked, "are not popular assemblies frequently subject to the impulses of rage, resentment, jealousy, avarice, and of other irregular and violent propensities?"

THE IRON LAW OF OLIGARCHY   Madison's approach was less impassioned and more analytical. With the membership of the House of Representatives to stand at 65 and with the odds that it would grow in size, there was reason to believe that it would be manipulated by an oligarchic elite. His statement of this "law," in No. 58, is as follows:

> In all legislative assemblies the greater the number composing them may be, the fewer will be the men who will in fact direct their proceedings. In the first place, the more numerous any assembly may be, of whatever characters composed, the greater is known to be the ascendancy of passion over reason. In the next place, the larger the number, the greater will be the proportion of members with limited information and of weak capacities. Now, it is precisely on characters of this description that the eloquence and address of the few are known to act with all their force. . . . On the same principle, the more multitudinous a representative assembly may be rendered, the more it will partake of the infirmities incident to collective meetings of the people. Ignorance will be the dupe of cunning, and passion the slave of sophistry and declamation. The people can never err more than in supposing that by multiplying their representatives beyond a certain limit they strengthen the barrier against the government of a few.

Hamilton and Madison both harbored the fear that the House of Representatives might become an indoor mob, its members listening rapt as their demogogic leaders harangued them to a fever pitch. Legislation could be enacted on impulse, based on ignorance, and productive of injustice.

What can and must be said is that the major conclusions of the *Federalist* authors may have been correct, but they were wrong in predicting the form that oligarchic rule would take in the House of Representatives. There is, indeed, an elite in the lower chamber and it does indeed make the major decisions on legislation. But these leaders are far from being fiery orators who stir the emotions of the rank and file. On the contrary, they are party leaders—especially the Speaker

—and committee chairmen who rise to power not so much because they have extraordinary talent but rather because of their seniority. The power that comes to them is not due to personal ambition but instead to the fact that decision-making has to be centralized in a few hands if business is to get done at all in a large legislative chamber. The "iron law of oligarchy" foreseen by Hamilton and Madison *has* come to pass in the House of Representatives, but the oligarchs are not mob leaders. They are, on the contrary, rather ordinary men who sit at the organizational controls. The power they hold is less eye-catching than that of the demagogue, but it is more effective in the long run. Nor can these men easily be removed or replaced. For even if they were deposed, others just like them would have to step into their positions.

ARISTOCRACY IN A DEMOCRACY The authors of *The Federalist* started with the assumption that original sin pervaded all of society, that all men were imperfect in reason and prone to perversity. This theory apparently applied to the rich as well as to the poor, to the educated as well as to the ignorant, to rulers as well as to the ruled. However, on at least one occasion Hamilton and Madison seemed to suggest that their strictures on human nature were not altogether universal in application. There might, in America, be some individuals who are less susceptible to irrationality and who are relatively immune to passion. Such a notion was clearly in Madison's mind when he discussed the "necessity of a well-constructed Senate" in No. 63. He wrote:

> An institution may be sometimes necessary as a defense to the people against their own temporary errors and delusions. As the cool and deliberate sense of the community ought, in all governments, and actually will, in all free governments, ultimately prevail over the views of its rulers; so there are particular moments in public affairs when the people, stimulated by some irregular passion, or some illicit advantage, or misled by the artful misrepresentations of interested men, may call for measures which they themselves will afterwards be the most ready to lament and condemn. In these critical moments, how salutary will be the interference of some temperate and respectable body of citizens, in order to check

> the misguided career and to suspend the blow medi-
> tated by the people against themselves, until reason,
> justice, and truth can regain their authority over the
> public mind?

In view of the prediction that the House of Representatives might
be excessive and intemperate in its behavior, it was Madison's hope that
the Senate would act as a counterbalance. Provisions contained in the
proposed constitution made manifest this intention. Members of the
upper chamber were to serve terms that were three times as long as
those of their colleagues below; they were to be selected by the state
legislatures rather than by popular election; and the smaller states
would, in the Senate, have the power that they lacked in the House.

The people must be protected from "their own temporary errors and
delusions" and the need for such protection assumes that the public
does not always know its own best interests. The people, Madison's
theory says, may *think* they know what they want. But in actual fact
they may be blind to their *real* needs. And so, out of necessity, will be
the House of Representatives. For this popular chamber will be forced
to reflect the momentary whims of its constituents. Therefore the Senate, indirectly elected and secure in its six-year tenure, will ignore the
"errors and delusions" of the public and correct the legislative exuber-
ance of the House of Representatives. Madison supposed that there
existed an identifiable group of "temperate and respectable" citizens and
that the Senate would be recruited from this superior group. Since the
time of the writing of *The Federalist* there has been a great deal of
controversy over whether the Senate has actually checked tyrannical
bills that may have been passed by the House of Representatives. It
can be argued that senators, perhaps because since 1913 they have been
popularly elected, are swept along by the same currents of public
opinion as are the representatives. Indeed, it is not as easy as one
might think to compile a list of instances where the lower chamber
has acted rashly and has then been checked by its senior colleague. In
addition, the "iron law of oligarchy" that operates in the House of
Representatives has provided a set of self-controls independent of those
that might be exercised by the Senate.

What can be said for Madison's prediction is that senators have shown
themselves to be "superior" in a number of ways when compared with
members of the House of Representatives. They are less parochial because a man who aspires to the upper chamber must appeal to a broader
constituency. He must have the intelligence to understand not simply

one locality and one set of interests, but the habits and interests of a wide spectrum of citizens. This is particularly true at the nominating stage, when a would-be senator must make a persuasive case for his candidacy to the statewide leadership of his party. However, the "superiority" of the senators over the representatives provides not so much a hedge against tyrannical laws as an infusion of more intelligence and sophistication into the legislative process. And this end, quite obviously, is one that Hamilton and Madison fervently sought to secure.

PRESIDENT AND SUPREME COURT

The analysis of the Presidency fell to Hamilton, and to this discussion he brought the ideas that characterize his entire approach to politics. If Madison wanted a Senate composed of superior men, Hamilton was no less concerned to see the Presidency filled with the best person America had to offer. In No. 68 he explained how the electoral college—which was to select the Chief Executive—would ensure that quality would be the uppermost consideration. The meetings of the electors in the various states would be private affairs, affording "as little opportunity as possible to tumult and disorder." The electors would meet separately at their respective state capitals, and would not foregather in a large and possibly discordant convention that might occur were they to make their decision collectively. All in all, the process of selecting a President would be so hedged that only the most eminent citizens would be considered, let alone chosen. Hamilton continued in No. 68:

> The process of election affords a moral certainty that the office of President will never fall to the lot of any man who is not in an eminent degree endowed with the requisite qualifications. Talents for low intrigue, the little arts of popularity, may alone suffice to elevate a man to the first honors in a single state; but it will require other talents, and a different kind of merit, to establish him in the esteem and confidence of the whole Union, or of so considerable a portion of it as would be necessary to make him a successful candidate for the distinguished office of President of the United States. It will not be too strong to say that there will be a constant probability of seeing the station filled by characters pre-eminent for ability and virtue.

When Hamilton said that a presidential candidate would have to be of sufficient stature to gain the "esteem and confidence of the whole Union," he meant not that he would be the choice of a nationwide electorate but rather of the members of the Electoral College to be appointed by the state legislatures. Since the early decades of the nineteenth century the electors have felt obliged to cast their ballots for the man who has most support in the popular elections in their states. It is worth taking a moment to speculate whether the country has had fewer eminent men as President since the electors stopped using their own judgment and began to reflect public sentiment. The change came in the 1820s, and most commentators would acknowledge that the Presidents prior to that time—Washington, Adams, Jefferson, Madison, and Monroe—presented an unbroken array of first-class talent. There have been great men in the White House since the 1820s, but there have also been incompetents and nonentities. What would have happened had the members of the electoral college continued to exercise a judgment independent of the popular vote? The answer to this question is to be found in the kind of man the state legislatures would appoint as electors. There is strong reason to believe that they would be professional politicians rather than citizens who stood "above" party, that they would be products of organization politics rather than disinterested statesmen. Considering the composition of state legislatures, the electors would be preponderantly rural and mainly conservative. It is highly doubtful if they would have elected as President a Theodore Roosevelt, a Woodrow Wilson, a Franklin D. Roosevelt, or even a Dwight Eisenhower. In other words, it has been the development of the popular election for President—with all its "tumult and disorder"—that has given the country not a few chief executives with a national perspective. Hamilton was correct in saying that the President must be a figure who transcends regional loyalties and interests. But it was Madison who saw that the democratic process in a large nation would cancel out parochial tendencies and, by means of conference and compromise, produce leaders of stature.

AN ENERGETIC EXECUTIVE   The stress that Hamilton placed on national authority led him, quite naturally, to advocate a strong and purposive President. "Energy in the executive is a leading character in the definition of good government," he said in No. 70. And, he continued, "the ingredients which constitute energy in the executive are unity, duration, an adequate provision for its support, and competent powers." The first two of these "ingredients" are more or less self-explanatory. A unified executive means that the President is to be the sole master of his household. He must not be forced to share his authority with another agency or individual within the executive branch. As far as duration is concerned, he will have a four-year term of office and the chances are good that he will be reelected for a second four-year term. Having one man serve eight years as Chief Executive of a country was an unusual occurrence for that time, but Hamilton realized that a powerful President would have to have an extended term if he were to inaugurate and carry out the programs the young nation so sorely needed for its survival. The third ingredient, "adequate provision," acknowledged that the President must be suitably compensated. While he is never going to be the best-paid man in the country, he must nevertheless be financially independent so that he is relieved of personal problems and is beholden to no one. George Washington's salary was $25,000 per year in 1789 and John Kennedy's was $100,000 (plus $50,-000 for personal expenses) in 1963. It so happens that neither the first nor the thirty-fifth President needed the salary he was given, but most of those who came between them did.

But Hamilton's chief interest lay in the political powers of the President, and he devoted five papers, beginning with No. 73, to a discussion of the ways the Chief Executive could use his constitutional authority. He was to have the right to veto legislation, to serve as commander in chief, to negotiate treaties, to pardon offenders, to appoint public officials, and to address the Congress. The last power is given but cursory attention. In No. 77 Hamilton briefly mentioned the President's "giving information to Congress of the state of the Union" and his "recommending to their consideration such measures as he shall judge expedient." Yet the energetic President envisioned by Hamilton would necessarily become a legislative leader. He would have to draw up a program that was uniquely his own, and not only "recommend" it to the Congress but use all the resources of his office to see that the Senate and the House of Representatives complied with his demands. Were he simply to administer whatever laws the Congress decided that it wanted to pass, he would be little more than a glorified clerk. Hamilton's intention was made clear in No. 11 when he asserted that it was government's responsibility to promote business enterprise and to develop the nation's economy. An ambitious program like this would come only from an energetic executive. For a great deal of presidential energy would be needed to persuade a legislature dominated by rural senators and representatives who would have little sympathy for industrialization and the prospect of increased urbanization. Hamilton confined his analysis to the constitutional powers of the President and he did not enter into a discussion of the practical techniques a chief executive would have to use if he wanted to secure the passage of his legislative program. But this can hardly be construed as a criticism of Hamilton. For more than 170 years Presidents have sought to discover the most effective ways and means of becoming legislative leaders. Some have been relatively successful, others have been failures, and still others have abdicated the role completely. But none have mastered this feat in all its complexities and particulars.

GUARDIAN OF THE CONSTITUTION   Of the three branches of government, the Supreme Court received least attention in both *The Federalist* and the Constitution itself. The judicial powers of the Supreme Court were described and there was no real controversy over its authority to hear appeals from the state courts. But was the Supreme Court to have a political role as well? Here the proposed constitution was silent. While the checks and balances running from the legislature to the executive received extensive consideration, the Supreme Court was apparently to be a junior partner. It was therefore something of a bombshell when, in No. 78, Hamilton departed from a simple explication of the text of the Constitution and began to describe the Supreme Court's role in relation to the Congress. He pointed out that the judiciary must be a completely independent department and that this independence was required for political reasons. He wrote:

> The complete independence of the courts of justice is peculiarly essential in a limited constitution. By a limited constitution, I understand one which contains certain specified exceptions to the legislative authority; such for instance, as that it shall pass no bills of attainder, no *ex post facto* laws, and the like. Limitations of this kind can be preserved in practice no other way than through the medium of courts of justice, whose duty it must be to declare all acts contrary to the manifest tenor of the constitution void. Without this, all the reservations of particular rights or privileges would amount to nothing. . . .

> There is no position which depends on clearer
> principles than that every act of a delegated author-
> ity, contrary to the tenor of the commission under
> which it is exercised, is void. No legislative act,
> therefore, contrary to the constitution, can be valid.
> . . . Where the will of the legislature, declared
> in its statutes, stands in opposition to that of the
> people, declared in the constitution, the judges ought
> to be governed by the latter rather than the former.
> They ought to regulate their decisions by the funda-
> mental laws rather than by those which are not
> fundamental.

An appointed body of five men (nine men now), holding office for
life, was to have the power to nullify acts passed by lawmakers elected
by the people or their representatives. A nondemocratic tribunal, in
other words, would be able to override the branch of government
chosen by and responsible to the electorate. How could judicial
supremacy be justified? Hamilton's reasoning was, first, that the Constitution was the "fundamental" law of the land and that its provisions
stood on higher ground than any statutes passed by the legislature.
And, second, he asserted that the Constitution, once adopted, would express the "real" will of the people. That is, acts of Congress might
claim to represent the public will, but they might actually be expressing the transitory whims and momentary passions of the electorate. The
Constitution, however, embodied the lasting political values of the
American people.

Since the publication of No. 78 and the initial application of judicial review a decade and a half later by John Marshall in *Marbury v.
Madison*, there has been endless debate on the powers of the judicial
branch. Hamilton's prediction, in No. 81, was that members of the
Supreme Court would be outstanding legal scholars, men "selected for
their knowledge of the laws, acquired by long and laborious study."
These men, presumably, would rise above partisan politics and the
everyday clash of interests. They would, so it was supposed, interpret
the Constitution coolly and dispassionately; and if they declared an
act of Congress void they would do so because it clearly ran counter
to the fundamental law as expressed in that document. But there is
reason to suspect that there was more on Hamilton's mind than legal
consistency. His interests were in establishing national authority and

in encouraging industrial growth, and in all likelihood he intended that the Supreme Court would aid in this mission by overriding acts of a rural and agrarian Congress tempted to hamper these objectives. To be sure this strategy is not explicitly stated in *The Federalist*, but it can be inferred from Hamilton's major assumptions concerning the course of American development.

THE COURT'S CONSTITUENCY To challenge a popularly elected legislature requires both courage and power. From 1803 until 1937 the Supreme Court exercised Hamilton's mandate, striking down approximately 80 acts of Congress. It was able to do this largely because it had a series of powerful "constituencies" upon which it could rely for support. For even though it was an appointed body, the Supreme Court was able to gain support of important groups in society which were prepared to defend its authority over that of the Congress. These constituencies were, first, the mercantile and financial interests of the Northeast, later the slaveholding interests of the South, and finally the burgeoning entrepreneurial interests that dominated the nation's economy from the close of the Civil War until the Depression of the 1930s. This was the kind of support Hamilton hoped would emerge for an independent judiciary. And in major particulars his forecast was a correct one for the first century and a half of the Republic's life. However, since the days of the New Deal the Supreme Court has been isolated rather than independent. It no longer has behind it a coherent and identifiable constituency; there is no major group of power and prestige to defend it against its detractors. For this reason it has had to scale down any political pretensions it might currently have.

It is not surprising that in the last quarter of a century the Supreme Court has not nullified an important act of Congress. It has exercised some control, for example, over the procedures used in congressional investigations but it has not challenged the legislature in the realm of public policy. The Supreme Court has, in short, restricted its use of judicial review to voiding acts of state legislative bodies. Most of the justices realize that were they to attempt to override the Congress on significant policy issues, they would be faced with a counterattack against which they would have no effective defense. The recent isolation of the judicial branch is an important problem and it is one of the unanticipated consequences of the fragmentation of power in American politics.

FREEDOM AND AUTHORITY

The proposed constitution sought to reconcile some of the major values facing modern government. The authors of *The Federalist* built their theory on a conception of society that was not beyond the powers of mortal men to attain. Madison was speaking both for himself and for Hamilton when he said in No. 51:

> But what is government itself but the greatest of all reflections on human nature? If men were angels, no government would be necessary. If angels were to govern men, neither external nor internal controls on government would be necessary. In framing a government which is to be administered by men over men, the great difficulty lies in this: you must first enable the government to control the governed; and in the next place oblige it to control itself.

Hamilton's great concern was to establish a government capable of controlling the governed, one that would allow for purposive and energetic leadership. His goal was to secure a strong national authority, and to this end he hoped to underpin the new republic with the support of a powerful class in society. Madison's concern, on the other hand, was to establish a government that would have the internal mechanisms to control itself. To achieve this objective he defended the principles of federalism, separation of powers, and social pluralism. He was less interested in establishing a class base for the political system and more in seeing that a wide variety of interests were represented in the governmental process.

On a superficial reading it would seem that Hamilton's and Madison's aims could only run counter to each other. For would not Hamilton's goal of unified national power be upset by Madison's checks and balances and Federal-state rivalries? The response must be that while differing in these important particulars, both *Federalist* authors were dedicated to the ideas of a united nation and individual freedom. But even on the question of freedom they were not wholly in agreement. For Hamilton, freedom spelled the right of the businessman to make money and invest it in productive enterprise. For Madison, it was the freedom of individuals and minorities to express their opinions and to worship

God without having these rights abridged by an intolerant majority. Both authors shared misgivings about majority rule and the institutions of popular democracy. There can be no overlooking the tensions embodied in *The Federalist*. Indeed it was Madison himself, in No. 10, who said, "As long as the reason of man continues fallible, and he is at liberty to exercise it, different opinions will be formed."

Review Questions

1. What were to be the functions and characteristics of the House of Representatives?

2. What is the "iron law of oligarchy"?

3. In what ways would the Senate differ from the House of Representatives?

4. What kind of men did Hamilton think ought to be selected for the Presidency?

5. In what sense was the Supreme Court to be the guardian of the Constitution?

6. Did Hamilton and Madison agree or differ in their fundamental aims?

For Further Reading

THE STUDY OF POLITICS

CATLIN, GEORGE: *Systematic Politics*, University of Toronto Press, Toronto, Canada, 1962.

LASSWELL, HAROLD, and ABRAHAM KAPLAN: *Power and Society*, Yale University Press, New Haven, Conn., 1950.

STORING, HERBERT (ed.): *Essays on the Scientific Study of Politics*, Holt, Rinehart and Winston, Inc., New York, 1962.

VAN DYKE, VERNON: *Political Science: A Philosophical Analysis*, Stanford University Press, Stanford, Calif., 1960.

YOUNG, ROLAND (ed.): *Approaches to the Study of Politics*, Northwestern University Press, Evanston, Ill., 1958.

THE WESTERN TRADITION

EBENSTEIN, WILLIAM: *An Introduction to Political Philosophy*, Holt, Rinehart and Winston, Inc., New York, 1952.

HACKER, ANDREW: *Political Theory: Philosophy, Ideology, Science*, The Macmillan Company, New York, 1961.

SABINE, GEORGE: *A History of Political Theory*, Holt, Rinehart and Winston, Inc., New York, 1961.

STRAUSS, LEO: *What Is Political Philosophy?* The Free Press of Glencoe, New York, 1959.

WOLIN, SHELDON: *Politics and Vision*, Little, Brown and Company, Boston, 1960.

AMERICAN ORIGINS

BRANT, IRVING: *James Madison: Father of the Constitution*, The Bobbs-Merrill Company, Inc., Indianapolis, 1950.

DIETZE, GOTTFRIED: *The Federalist: A Classic on Federalism and Free Government*, The Johns Hopkins Press, Baltimore, 1960.

FARRAND, MAX: *The Framing of the Constitution*, Yale University Press, New Haven, Conn., 1913.

HACKER, LOUIS M.: *Alexander Hamilton in the American Tradition*, McGraw-Hill Book Company, Inc., New York, 1957.

VAN DOREN, CARL: *The Great Rehearsal*, The Viking Press, Inc., New York, 1948.

AMERICAN INSTITUTIONS

BAILEY, STEPHEN, and HOWARD SAMUEL: *Congress at Work,* Holt, Rinehart and Winston, Inc., New York, 1952.

CORWIN, EDWARD: *The President: Office and Powers,* New York University Press, New York, 1957.

FREUND, PAUL: *On Understanding the Supreme Court,* Little, Brown and Company, Boston, 1949.

MASON, ALPHEUS, and WILLIAM BEANEY: *The Supreme Court in a Free Society,* Prentice-Hall, Inc., Englewood Cliffs, N.J., 1959.

ROSSITER, CLINTON: *The American Presidency,* Harvest Books, Harcourt, Brace & World, Inc., New York, 1960.

WESTIN, ALAN (ed.): *The Uses of Power: Seven Cases in American Politics,* Harcourt, Brace & World, Inc., 1961.

WHITE, WILLIAM S.: *Citadel: The Story of the United States Senate,* Harper & Row, Publishers, Incorporated, New York, 1957.

Index